AAT

Qualifications and Credit Framework (QCF)
LEVEL 3 DIPLOMA IN ACCOUNTING

WORKBOOK

Spreadsheet Software

2010 Edition

First edition July 2010

ISBN 9780 7517 8583 8

British Library Cataloguing-in-Publication Data
A catalogue record for this book is available from the British
Library

Published by

BPP Learning Media Ltd
BPP House
Aldine Place
London
W12 8AA

www.bpp.com/learningmedia

Printed in the United Kingdom by
Martins the Printers, Berwick upon Tweed

Your learning materials, published by BPP Learning Media Ltd,
are printed on paper sourced from sustainable, managed forests.

CONTENTS

Chapters and chapter tasks

*Study <u>either</u> Chapter 1 and 2 (Microsoft Office Excel 2007) <u>or</u>
Chapters 3 and 4 (Microsoft Office Excel 2003)*

Spreadsheet practice

INTRODUCTION

This is a time of great change for the AAT. From 1 July 2010 the AAT's assessments will fall within the **Qualifications and Credit Framework** and most papers will be assessed by way of an on demand **computer based assessment**. BPP Learning Media has reacted to this change by investing heavily to produce new ground-breaking, market-leading resources.

In particular, our **new suite of online resources** ensures that students are prepared for online testing by means of an online environment where tasks mimic the style of the AAT's assessment tasks.

The BPP range of resources comprises:

- **Texts**, covering all the knowledge and understanding needed by students, with numerous illustrations of 'how it works', practical examples and tasks for you to use to consolidate your learning. The majority of tasks within the texts have been written in an interactive style that reflects the style of the online tasks the AAT will set. Texts are available in our traditional paper format and, in addition, as E books which can be downloaded to your PC or laptop.

- **Question Banks**, including additional learning questions plus the AAT's practice assessment and a number of other full practice assessments. Full answers to all questions and assessments, prepared by BPP Learning Media Ltd, are included. For the first time our question banks are available in an online environment which mimics the AAT's testing environment. This enables you to familiarise yourself with the environment in which you will be tested

- **Passcards,** which are handy pocket sized revision tools designed to fit in a handbag or briefcase to enable you to revise anywhere at anytime. All major points are covered in the passcards which have been designed to assist you in consolidating knowledge

- **Workbooks,** which have been designed to cover the units that are assessed by way of project/case study. The workbooks contain many practical tasks to assist in the learning process and also a sample assessment or project to work through.

- **Lecturers' resources**, providing a further bank of tasks, answers and full practice assessments for classroom use, available separately only to lecturers whose colleges adopt BPP Learning Media material. The lecturers resources are available in both paper format and online in E format.

This Workbook, for Spreadsheet Software, has been written specifically to ensure complete yet concise coverage of the AAT's new learning outcomes and assessment criteria. It is fully up to date as at June 2010 and reflects both the AAT's unit guide and practice assessment.

Each chapter contains:

- Clear, step by step explanations of the topics

- Hands-on, interactive exercises and illustrations

- Test your learning questions, with answers provided at the end of the book

The emphasis in all tasks and questions is on the practical application of the skills acquired.

If you have any comments about this book, please e-mail suedexter@bpp.com or write to Sue Dexter, Publishing Director, BPP Learning Media Ltd, BPP House, Aldine Place, London W12 8AA.

ASSESSMENT STRATEGY

Spreadsheet Software (SPSW) is assessed at Level 3.

The unit may be assessed either using Workplace Evidence (which is locally assessed by a centre) or by completing the Computer Based Assessment (which is set centrally and assessed by the AAT).

The assessment is approximately 1 hours and 30 minutes.

- **Part 1** contains several short written tasks which must be completed in one session

- **Part 2** consists of an assignment asking the learner to input data into a spreadsheet and produce charts

- **Part 3** contains two multiple choice questions

The purpose of the assessment is to allow the learner to demonstrate the skills and knowledge necessary to use spreadsheet software at level 3.

The assessment is designed to allow the use of any spreadsheet software package and is in the form of a project, which comprises three parts that can be completed over a period of time.

Competency

The assessment material will normally be provided by the AAT, delivered online and assessed locally. Candidates can provide workplace evidence.

Learners will be required to demonstrate competence in all sections of the assessment.

For the purpose of assessment the competency level for AAT assessment is set at 70 per cent.

The Level Descriptor below describes the ability and skills students at this level must successfully demonstrate to achieve competence.

QCF Level descriptor	Summary
	Achievement at Level 3 reflects the ability to identify and use relevant understanding, methods and skills to complete tasks and address problems that, while well defined, have a measure of complexity. It includes taking responsibility for initiating and completing tasks and procedures as well as exercising autonomy and judgement within limited parameters. It also reflects awareness of different perspectives or approaches within an area of study or work.
	Knowledge and understanding
	■ Use factual, procedural and theoretical understanding to complete tasks and address problems that, while well defined, may be complex and non-routine
	■ Interpret and evaluate relevant information and ideas
	■ Be aware of the nature of the area of study or work
	■ Have awareness of different perspectives or approaches within the area of study or work
	Application and action
	■ Address problems that, while well defined, may be complex and non routine
	■ Identify, select and use appropriate skills, methods and procedures
	■ Use appropriate investigation to inform actions
	■ Review how effective methods and actions have been
	Autonomy and accountability
	■ Take responsibility for initiating and completing tasks and procedures, including, where relevant, responsibility for supervising or guiding others
	■ Exercise autonomy and judgement within limited parameters

AAT UNIT GUIDE

Spreadsheet Software (SPSW)

Introduction

Please read this document in conjunction with the standards for all relevant units.

This unit is about the learner having the ability to use a software application designed to record data in rows and columns; perform calculations with numerical data and also present the information using charts and graphs.

Learning objectives

An advanced user can select and use a wide range of advanced spreadsheet software tools and techniques to produce, present and check spreadsheets that are complex and non-routine.

Spreadsheet software tools and techniques will be defined as 'advanced' because:

- the range of data entry, manipulation and outputting techniques will be complex and non-routine

- the tools, formulas and functions needed to analyse and interpret the required information requires complex and non-routine knowledge and understanding (for example, data restrictions, data validation using formula, pivot tables, data maps)

- the user will take full responsibility for setting up and developing the functionality of the spreadsheet

The purpose of the unit

This unit has been designed by e-skills to describe the skills and competencies of an **intermediate** spreadsheet user.

The use of spreadsheet software tools and techniques are defined as 'intermediate' because:

- the range of data entry, manipulation and outputting techniques will be multi-step and at times non-routine or unfamiliar

- the tools, formulas and functions needed to analyse and interpret the data requires knowledge and understanding (for example, mathematical, logical, statistical or financial)

- the user will take some responsibility for setting up or developing the structure and functionality of the spreadsheet.

Learning outcomes

There are three learning outcomes for this unit, the learner will...

(1) Use a spreadsheet to enter, edit and organise numerical and other data

(2) Select and use appropriate formulas and data analysis tools and techniques to meet requirements

(3) Use tools and techniques to present, and format and publish spreadsheet information

QCF Unit Spreadsheet Software (SPSW)		
Learning Outcome	Assessment Criteria	Covered in Chapter
Use a spreadsheet to enter, edit and organise numerical and other data	Identify what numerical and other information is needed in the spreadsheet and how it should be structured	1 & 3
	Enter and edit numerical and other data accurately	1 & 3
	Combine and link data from different sources	1 & 3
	Store and retrieve spreadsheet files effectively, in line with local guidelines and conventions where available	2 & 4
Select and use formulas and data analysis tools and techniques to meet requirements	Explain what methods can be used to summarise, analyse and interpret spreadsheet data and when to use them	1 – 4
	Select and use a wide range of appropriate functions and formulas to meet calculation requirements	1 – 4
	Select and use a range of tools and techniques to analyse and interpret data to meet requirements	2 & 4
	Select and use forecasting tools and techniques	2 & 4
Use tools and techniques to present, and format and publish spreadsheet information	Explain how to present and format spreadsheet information effectively to meet needs	1 – 4
	Select and use appropriate tools and techniques to format spreadsheet cells, rows, columns and worksheets effectively	1 – 4
	Select and use appropriate tools and techniques to generate, develop and format charts and graphs	1 – 4
	Select and use appropriate page layout to present, print and publish spreadsheet information	1 & 3
	Explain how to find and sort out any errors in formulas	2 & 4
	Check spreadsheet information meets needs, using IT tools and making corrections as necessary	2 & 4
	Use auditing tools to identify and respond appropriately to any problems with spreadsheets	2 & 4

The following are **examples** of what the learner will be required to be familiar with. However, this is intended only as a guide to the most common areas to be assessed.

- The learner will be familiar with the component parts of a spreadsheet including - workbook, worksheet, column, row, cell, active cell, tab, page and panes/windows.
- The learner will be able to use the following functions in editing and entering data across single or multiple cells – insert, delete, input/amend text and numerical data, copy, cut, paste, paste special, clear and find and replace.
- The learner will be able to reorganise data in different formats and link, embed and import/export data from a different source.
- The learner will be able to use the following functions – Save, Save as, file name/rename, folder name, rename, password protect files, backup and archive information.
- The learner will be able to use the following functions in analysing and interpreting data - addition, subtraction, multiplication, division, sum, percentages, parentheses, Pivot Table, Consolidation, Sort data, Filter Data, Data restriction, Data Validation, Find and replace, Look Up, If, And, Auto sum (count, max, min, sum, average), relative references, absolute references and Date (today, now, day/month/year).
- The learner will be able to lock and hide cells.
- The learner will be able to use the analysis tools within the spreadsheet. This can include, but not be restricted to, rank and percentile, moving averages and histograms.
- The learner will be able to forecast using trend lines within the spreadsheet.
- Learners will be able to use the following formatting tools - Fixed decimal, 1000 separator, "£", formatting percentages, applying the accounting double underline to cells, text alignment, font and font size, cell justification, borders, shading, merge cells, conditional formatting, page setup (margins, orientation, print area) and be able to print formula.
- Learners will be able to insert and delete columns, rows, cells and to change the row height, column width.
- Learners be able to hide and unhide cells and protect spreadsheets/cells.
- Learners will be able to produce and label charts and graphs (bar, line, pie, scatter, doughnut, bubble).
- Learners will know how to use page layouts to present data and scale information for printing purposes.
- Learners will check spreadsheets for errors in content and in formulas using the following functions - error checking, trace error and circular references and formula auditing.
- Learners will ensure that the information contained within the spreadsheet meets the needs of the recipient.

Delivery guidance

The learner must be able to:

- Use existing spreadsheets,
- Use spreadsheet templates, and also
- Produce individual spreadsheets to meet certain requirements.

Therefore they will need to:

- Identify what data (numerical and text) should be included within the spreadsheet and

- How the spreadsheet should be structured.

Spreadsheet structure covers:

- The use of spreadsheet templates for routine work and also

- The production of a spreadsheet for a particular reason.

There should be a planned structure to the spreadsheet and the design and layout should be appropriate to the task.

Learners should know and be able to work with all component parts of spreadsheets:

- Cells
- Rows
- Columns
- Tabs
- Pages
- Charts
- Workbooks
- Worksheets and
- Windows

The learner has to be able to enter and edit data accurately. This could include numerical and textual data.

They must be able to:

- Insert data into single and multiple cells
- Clear cells
- Edit cell contents
- Replicate data
- Copy
- Paste
- Find and replace
- Add and delete rows and columns
- Use absolute and relative cell references and
- Add data and text to a chart

They should also be able to hide and protect cells, and link data.

Learners must be able to store and retrieve spreadsheets – therefore they could be assessed on using:

- Folders (eg create and name) and
- Files, eg
    - Create
    - Name
    - Open
    - Save
    - Save as
    - Print
    - Close
    - Find
    - Share

They should also be able to:

- Use version control
- Import/export files into other documents and also
- Archive information (backup and restore)

Learners need to be able to use a wide range of formulae and functions to complete calculations; they should be able to use the design of formulas to meet calculation requirements. These could include mathematical, statistical, financial, conditional, look-up, and logical functions.

They must be able to use a range of techniques to summarise data and then analyse and interpret the results, These can be assessed and include the following summarising tools:

- Totals and sub-totals
- Sorting of a cell range
- Filter rows and columns
- Data restriction
- Tables
- Graphs and charts
- Simple pivot tables and charts

The learner can be assessed on their judgment of when and how to use these methods.

Learners can be assessed on using the tools, formulas and functions (for example, data restrictions, data validation using formula and pivot tables) needed to analyse the information within a spreadsheet.

The learner must then be able to develop the spreadsheets by using forecasting techniques:

- What-if scenarios,
- Goal seek and
- Data tables may be assessed.

Spreadsheets then need to be prepared for publication or sharing with others. The learner should be able to format spreadsheet contents (cells, rows and columns) to ensure that they meet a competent standard and are easy to read. This can include:

- Height and width and shading for rows and columns and for cells
- Formatting for numbers or text
- Currency
- Percentages
- Number of decimal place
- Dates
- Font
- Alignment
- Colour
- Shading and borders and
- Conditional formatting alignment of cell content

Learners must be able to produce the information within the spreadsheet in different formats. They could be assessed on choosing the most appropriate way to display information.

Charts must be correctly labelled (title, axis titles, axis scale and include a legend). All chart types may be assessed (bar, pie, bubble, doughnut, line and scatter graphs and may also include custom types, eg 2 graphs types on 1 axis and pivot table reports).

Learners should be able to change the chart type; move and resize a chart and annotate the chart as needed.

To present print and publish information the learner must ensure that spreadsheet is displayed in the best possible way and adjust the page set up, if necessary, for printing. This includes choosing:

- The font size
- The orientation (portrait or landscape)
- Margins
- Header and footer
- Page breaks
- Page numbering and
- Including a date/ time stamp

Learners will need to check the spreadsheets for any errors. This should include:

- Accuracy of numbers and any text

- Accuracy of results

- Correcting errors in formulas

- Checking the layout and format validity

- Using formulae to determine valid entries for cells, the validity, relevance and accuracy of analysis and the interpretation of calculations and results.

Errors, once identified, must be rectified and the learner's ability to do this can be assessed. The learner should be able to:

- Use the help facility
- Sort out errors in formulas (use audit formulas to check for errors)
- Identify and correct errors in circular references, calculations and results

They should also be able to validate data and locate and remove invalid data.

Non-assessable items

Macros will not be assessed.

SPREADSHEET SOFTWARE

Do students have to use Microsoft Excel to complete this Unit?

No. Students **do not** have to use Microsoft Excel (Excel) in their AAT Spreadsheet Software assessment.

The AAT recognise that a variety of productivity software packages are available and can be used. The only stipulation the AAT make is that the package used must be capable of performing the procedures outlined in the learning outcomes and assessment criteria.

Do students need access to Excel software to use this book?

Students that don't have Excel software may still pick up some useful information from this book.

However, those students with access to Excel will find it easier to work through the practical exercises than users of other accounting software packages.

Why does this Workbook refer to Excel 2003 and Excel 2007?

To explain and demonstrate the skills required in this Unit, it is necessary to provide practical examples and exercises. This requires the use of spreadsheet software.

This book provides examples taken from Excel 2003 and Excel 2007. Microsoft releases new versions of its software every few years, each time hoping to offer technical and user improvements. The basic functions are often the same.

Students should **study either chapters 1 and 2 (covering Excel 2007) or chapters 3 and 4 (covering Excel 2003)**.

What version do I need?

The illustrations in this book are taken from the latest versions at the time of publication (May 2010). These are Excel 2007 and 2003.

Microsoft will soon be releasing Excel 2010. It is expected that the majority of this book will remain valid for this version.

How do I buy Excel software?

Colleges

If this book is used by students in a college environment, the college will need either Excel 2003 or Excel 2007 installed on student computers.

Microsoft make Excel available to educational institutions at very reasonable rates. Colleges wanting to purchase Excel should **contact Microsoft**. In the UK, the number is 0870 60 70 800.

Individual students

Students are eligible to purchase Microsoft Excel at a discounted price. Visit Amazon's website and search for 'Microsoft Excel student edition'.

Are Excel data files available for use with this book?

Yes. Excel data files are provided either to provide a starting set of data or to show the results of an exercise. You will be given instructions for locating the relevant spreadsheet when you need it.

The spreadsheets referred to in the Workbook are available for download – type **www.bpp.com/aatspreadsheets** into your browser and follow the instructions provided.

chapter 1:
INTRODUCTION TO SPREADSHEETS (EXCEL 2007)

chapter coverage 📖

This chapter and the next introduce spreadsheets, using Excel 2007. Chapters 3 and 4 cover the same material using Excel 2003. You should study and work through *either* **chapters 1 and 2** *or* **chapters 3 and 4**, depending on the Excel software you have.

Spreadsheets have become indispensible tools for the presentation and analysis of accounting data. This chapter covers:

✎ An overview of spreadsheets.

✎ Essential basic skills that will allow you to move around a spreadsheet, enter and edit data, fill cells, and insert and delete columns and rows.

✎ An introduction to some of the many formulas and functions available within Excel 2007.

✎ Charts and graphs.

✎ Spreadsheet presentation and documentation including adding titles, clear labelling of rows and columns and appropriate formatting to help make the spreadsheet, and any charts in the spreadsheet, easy to read and interpret.

INTRODUCTION

The vast majority of people who work in an accounting environment are required to use spreadsheets to perform their duties. This fact is reflected in the AAT Standards, which require candidates to be able to produce clear, well-presented spreadsheets, that utilise appropriate spreadsheet functions and formulae.

WHAT IS A SPREADSHEET?

Before we start to use a spreadsheet, it is important to gain an overview of what a spreadsheet can do. Soon, you will be asked to open a spreadsheet and to work through some hands-on exercises.

A spreadsheet is essentially an electronic piece of paper divided into **rows** (horizontal) and **columns** (vertical). The rows are numbered 1, 2, 3 . . . etc and the columns lettered A, B, C . . . etc. Each individual area representing the intersection of a row and a column is called a 'cell'. A cell's address consists of its row and column reference. For example, in the spreadsheet below the word 'Jan' is in cell B2. The cell that the cursor is currently in or over is known as the 'active cell'. Active cells can be selected by clicking on them or using the arrow keys to move from one to the next.

The main examples of spreadsheet packages are Lotus 1-2-3 and Microsoft Excel. We will be referring to **Microsoft Excel**. The examples in this part of this book use **Excel 2007**. The second part of this book repeats the material but with reference to and using screen shots from **Excel 2003**.

A simple spreadsheet is shown below.

	A	B	C	D	E	F
1	BUDGETED SALES FIGURES					
2		Jan	Feb	Mar	Total	
3		£'000	£'000	£'000	£'000	
4	North	2,431	3,001	2,189	7,621	
5	South	6,532	5,826	6,124	18,482	
6	West	895	432	596	1,923	
7	Total	9,858	9,259	8,909	28,026	
8						

Why use spreadsheets?

Spreadsheets provide a tool for calculating, analysing and manipulating numerical data. Spreadsheets make the calculation and manipulation of data easier and quicker. For example, the spreadsheet above has been set up to calculate the totals **automatically**. If you changed your estimate of sales in February for the North region to £3,296, when you input this figure in cell C4 the totals (in E4, C7 and E7) would change automatically.

Uses of spreadsheets

Spreadsheets can be used for a wide range of tasks. Some common applications of spreadsheets are:

- Management accounts
- Cash flow analysis and forecasting
- Reconciliations
- Revenue analysis and comparison
- Cost analysis and comparison
- Budgets and forecasts

Spreadsheet software also provides basic database capabilities which allow simple records to be recorded, sorted and searched.

BASIC SKILLS

In this section we explain some **basic spreadsheet skills**.

You should read this section while sitting at a computer and trying out the skills we describe '**hands-on**'.

The menus

Start Microsoft Excel by double-clicking on the **Microsoft Office Excel 2007 (Excel) icon** or button on the computer desktop:

or by choosing Excel from the **Start** menu (possibly from within the **Microsoft Office** group).

The menu bars

When you first open Excel, you will see a tabbed toolbar, known as the 'Ribbon', which looks something like:

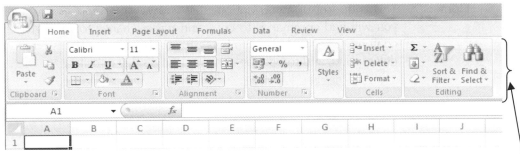

The full 'Ribbon'

Alternatively, it might look like:

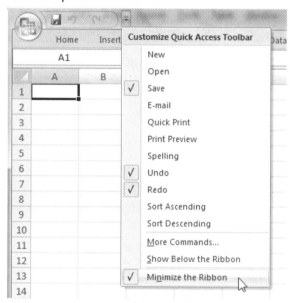

Here, the Ribbon has been minimised. This allows users more space in which to develop their spreadsheets, but for most of our work, we will keep the Ribbon visible. It can be made visible by clicking on the drop down arrow indicated above. This is part of the quick access toolbar.

Then uncheck 'Minimize the Ribbon' option. If you have a large screen available and maximise the Excel window, you will see more options in the Ribbon.

Related menu options are arranged into seven groups, or 'tabs', along the Ribbon:

Home: This is the set of menu options that you will use most often. Here you will find commands to copy and paste, change fonts, align cell contents, specify how numbers should be displayed, insert and delete rows, and to edit the contents and display of cells.

If you place your cursor over one of the icons on the menu and leave it there for a couple of seconds, a small help screen will appear. For example:

Try this for yourself now.

Insert: Allows tables, graphics, graphs and charts to be inserted into the spreadsheet. Some of these options are examined in detail later.

Page layout: Primarily deals with options available when you want to print out your spreadsheet.

Formulas: Allows you to insert functions such as those dealing with statistical or financial calculations. Also available here are powerful error checking facilities such as 'Trace Precedents' and 'Trace Dependents'. These allow you to see which other cells a cell value relies on or affects.

Data: This contains commands and options for the manipulation of data in simple Excel databases.

Review: Includes commands to spell-check and to protect cell contents by locking them. Also here is the option to 'draw' on the spreadsheet using your mouse so that errors or queries can be marked as though using a pen on a printout.

View: Provides options for how the spreadsheet appears on screen.

Have a look at the options provided by these top-line menu items. If you want to find out a little more, let your cursor linger over an icon until the small help call-out appears.

The Office button

The Office button is the circular, multi-coloured icon at the extreme top left of the spreadsheet. It is also a menu button and provides access to some important options.

Office button

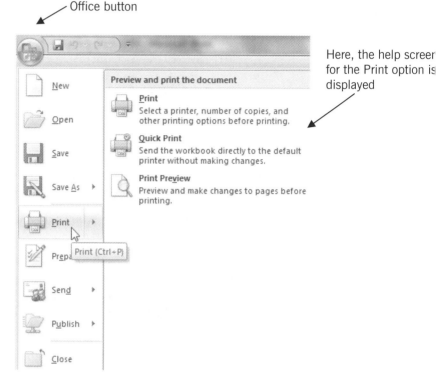

Here, the help screen for the Print option is displayed

Workbooks and worksheets

At the bottom left of the spreadsheet window you will see tabs which are known as **Worksheets**:

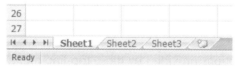

When **New** is selected from the Office button menu, a new **workbook** is created. The workbook consists of one or more **worksheets**. Think of worksheets as **pages** that make up the workbook. By default, a new Excel workbook starts out with three worksheets, although this can be changed (see later).

Worksheets can provide a convenient way of organising information. For example, consider a business consisting of three branches. Worksheets 2–4 could hold budget information separately for each branch. When entering formulae into cells it is possible to refer to cells in other worksheets within the workbook so it would then be possible for Worksheet 1 to show the totals of the budget information for the whole business. Effectively, a 'three dimensional' structure can be set up. We look at this in more detail later.

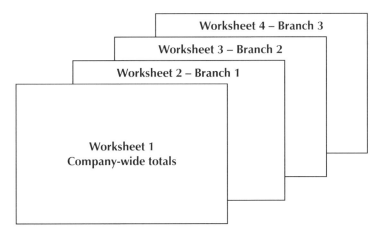

Opening an existing workbook

You can open an existing workbook file by using the menu commands **Office button>Open** and then navigating to the location of the file and double clicking on it.

If you open more than one workbook, each will open in a new window. To swap between open workbooks, click on the **Office button** and choose the workbook you want from the Recent documents list.

Closing a workbook

There are two ways to close a spreadsheet file:

(1)   Click the **Office button** and choose **Close** at the very bottom

(2)   Click on either the **'x'** in the top right hand corner of the window or the one just below it.

 OR

In both cases, if you have made any changes to the spreadsheet you will be asked if you want to save them. Choose **Yes** to save any changes (this will overwrite the existing file), **No** to close the file without saving any changes, or **Cancel** to return to the spreadsheet.

Cell contents

The contents of any cell can be one of the following:

(a)   **Text**. A text cell usually contains **words**. Numbers that do not represent numeric values for calculation purposes (eg a Part Number) may be entered in a way that tells Excel to treat the cell contents as text. To do this, enter an apostrophe before the number eg '451.

(b) **Values**. A value is a **number** that can be used in a calculation.

(c) **Formulae**. A formula **refers to other cells** in the spreadsheet, and performs some type of computation with them. For example, if cell C1 contains the formula =A1 – B1, cell C1 will display the result of the calculation subtracting the contents of cell B1 from the contents of cell A1. In Excel, a formula always begins with an equals sign: = . This alerts the program that what follows is a formula and not text or a value. There is a wide range of formulae and functions available.

Formulas and the formula bar

Open the workbook called ExcelExample1. This is one of the files available for download from www.bpp.com/aatspreadsheets. You can open a file by using the menu commands:

Office button>Open

then navigating to and double clicking on the file called ExcelExample1.

Note. Throughout this book we want spreadsheets to recalculate every time a figure is changed. This is the normal or default setting, so it is likely your spreadsheets already do this. But, if they don't, then:

(1) Click the **Microsoft Office Button** , click **Excel Options**, and then click the **Formulas** category.

(2) To recalculate all dependent formulas every time you make a change to a value, formula, or name, in the **Calculation options** section, under **Workbook Calculation**, click **Automatic**. This is the default calculation setting.

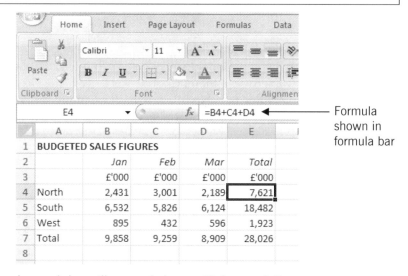

Formula shown in formula bar

You should see the worksheet illustrated above. Click on cell E4.

Look at the formula bar.

Note. If the formula bar is not visible, choose the **View** tab and check the **Formula Bar** box.

Note the important difference between:

(1)   What is shown in cell E4: 7,621

(2)   What is actually in cell E4: this is shown in the formula bar and it tells us that cell E4 is the result of adding together the contents of cells B4, C4 and D4

The formula bar allows you to see and edit the contents of the active cell. The bar also shows, on the left side, the cell address of the active cell (E4 in the example above).

Select different cells to be the active cell by using the up/down/right/left arrows on your keyboard or by clicking directly on the cell you want to be active. Look at what is in the cell and what is shown in the formula bar.

The **F5** key is useful for moving around within large spreadsheets. If you press the function key **F5**, a **Go To** dialogue box will allow you to specify the cell address you would like to move to. Try this out.

Also experiment by holding down Ctrl and pressing each of the direction arrow keys in turn to see where you end up. Try using the **Page Up** and **Page Down** keys and also try **Home** and **End** and Ctrl + these keys. Try **Tab** and **Shift + Tab**, too. These are all useful shortcuts for moving quickly from one place to another in a large spreadsheet.

Examples of spreadsheet formulae

Formulae in Microsoft Excel follow a specific syntax. All Excel formulae start with the equals sign =, followed by the elements to be calculated (the operands) and the calculation operators (such as +, -, /, *). Each operand can be a:

- Value that does not change (a constant value, such as the VAT rate)

- Cell or range reference to a range of cells

- Name (a named cell, such as 'VAT')

- Worksheet function (such as 'AVERAGE', which will work out the average value of defined values).

Formulae can be used to perform a variety of calculations. Here are some examples:

(a) =C4*5. This formula **multiplies** the value in C4 by 5. The result will appear in the cell holding the formula.

(b) =C4*B10. This **multiplies** the value in C4 by the value in B10.

(c) =C4/E5. This **divides** the value in C4 by the value in E5. * means multiply and / means divide by.

(d) =C4*B10 – D1. This **multiplies** the value in C4 by that in B10 and then subtracts the value in D1 from the result. Note that generally Excel will perform multiplication and division before addition or subtraction. If in any doubt, use brackets (parentheses): =(C4*B10) – D1.

(e) =C4*117.5%. This **adds** 17.5% to the value in C4. It could be used to calculate a price including 17.5% VAT.

(f) =(C4+C5+C6)/3. Note that the **brackets** mean Excel would perform the addition first. Without the brackets, Excel would first divide the value in C6 by 3 and then add the result to the total of the values in C4 and C5.

(g) = 2^2 gives you 2 **to the power** of 2, in other words 4. Likewise = 2^3 gives you 2 cubed and so on.

(h) = 4^(1/2) gives you the **square root** of 4. Likewise 27^(1/3) gives you the cube root of 27 and so on.

Displaying spreadsheet formulae

It is sometimes useful to see all formulae held in your spreadsheet to enable you to see how the spreadsheet works. There are two ways of making Excel **display the formulae** held in a spreadsheet.

(a) You can 'toggle' between the two types of display by pressing **Ctrl +`** (the latter is the key above the Tab key). Press **Ctrl +`** again to go back to the previous display.

(b) You can also click on **Formulas>Show Formulas** in the Ribbon.

The formulas for the spreadsheet we viewed earlier are shown below.

	A	B	C	D	E
1	BUDGETED S				
2		Jan	Feb	Mar	Total
3		£'000	£'000	£'000	£'000
4	North	2431	3001	2189	=B4+C4+D4
5	South	6532	5826	6124	=B5+C5+D5
6	West	895	432	596	=B6+C6+D6
7	Total	=B4+B5+B6	=C4+C5+C6	=D4+D5+D6	=E4+E5+E6

The importance of formulae

Look carefully at the example above and note which cells have formulae in them. It is important to realise that:

- If a cell contains a value, such as sales for North in January, then that data is entered as a number.

- If a cell shows the result of a calculation based on values in other cells, such as the total sales for January, then that cell contains a formula.

This is vital, because now if North's January sales were changed to, say, 2,500, the total would be automatically updated to show 9,927. Also the total for North would change to 7,690.

Try that out by clicking on cell B4 to make it active, then typing 2,500, followed by the Enter key. You should see both the totals change.

Now re-enter the original figure of 2,432 into cell B4.

Similarly, if a number is used more than once, for example a tax rate, it will be much better if the number is input to one cell only. Any other calculations making use of that value should refer to that cell. That way, if the tax rate changes, you only have to change it in one place in the spreadsheet (where it was originally entered) and any calculations making use of it will automatically change.

Your first function

In the example above, totals were calculated using a formula such as:

$$=+B4+C4+D4$$

That is fine provided there are not too many items to be included in the total. Imagine, the difficulty if you had to find the total of 52 weeks for a year. Adding up rows or columns is made much easier by using the SUM function. Instead of the formula above, we could place the following calculation in cell E4:

$$=SUM(B4:D4)$$

This produces the sum of all the cells in the range B4 to D4. Now it is much easier to add up a very long row of figures (for example, SUM(F5:T5)) or a very long column of figures (for example, SUM(B10:B60)).

There are three ways in which the SUM function can be entered. One way is simply to type =SUM(B4:D4) when E4 is the active cell. However, there is a more visual and perhaps more accurate way.

Make E4 the active cell by moving the cursor to it using the arrow keys or by clicking on it.

> Type =Sum(
>
> Click on cell B4
>
> Type a colon :
>
> Click on cell D4
>
> Close the bracket by typing)
>
> Press the Enter key

Another way is to use the AutoSum button, which we cover later.

Editing cell contents

Cell D5 of ExcelExample1 currently contains the value 6,124. If you wish to change the value in that cell from 6,124 to 6,154 there are four options (you have already used the first method).

(a) Activate cell D5, **type** 6,154 and press **Enter**.

 To undo this and try the next option press **Ctrl + Z**; this will always undo what you have just done (a very useful shortcut)

(b) **Double-click** in cell D5. The cell will keep its thick outline but you will now be able to see a vertical line flashing in the cell. You can move this line by using the direction arrow keys or the Home and the End keys. Move it to just after the 2, press the **backspace** key on the keyboard and then type 5. Then press **Enter**. (Alternatively, move the vertical line to just in front of the 2, press the **Delete** key on the keyboard, then type 5, followed by the **Enter** key).

 When you have tried this press **Ctrl + Z** to undo it.

(c) **Click once** before the number 6,124 in the formula bar. Again, you will get the vertical line which can be moved back and forth to allow editing as in (b) above.

(d) Activate cell D4 and press **F2** at the top of your keyboard. The vertical line cursor will be flashing in cell D4 at the *end* of the figures entered there and this can be used to edit the cell contents, as above.

Deleting cell contents

There are a number of ways to delete the contents of a cell:

(a) Make the cell the active cell and press the **Delete** button. The contents of the cell will disappear.

(b) Go to the **Editing** section on the **Home** tab of the Ribbon. Click on the **Clear** button and various options appear. Click **Clear Contents**. You can also achieve this by **right clicking** the cell and choosing **Clear contents**.

Any cell formatting (for example, cell colour or border) will not be removed when using either of these methods. To remove formatting click on the **Clear** button on the **Home** tab and select **Clear Formats**. If you want to remove the formatting *and* the contents, click **Clear All**.

Ranges of cells

A range of cells can occupy a single column or row or can be a rectangle of cells. The extent of a range is defined by the rectangle's top left cell reference and the bottom right cell reference. If the range is within a single row or column, it is defined by the references of the start and end cells.

Defining a range is very useful as you can then manipulate many cells at once rather than having to go to each one individually.

The following shows that a rectangular range of cells has been selected from C4 to D6. The range consists of three rows and two columns.

	A	B	C	D	E	F
1	BUDGETED SALES FIGURES					
2			Jan	Feb	Mar	Total
3			£'000	£'000	£'000	£'000
4	North		2,431	3,001	2,189	7,621
5	South		6,532	5,826	6,124	18,482
6	West		895	432	596	1,923
7	Total		9,858	9,259	8,909	28,026
8						
9						

There are several ways of selecting ranges. Try the following:

(1) Click on cell C4, but hold the mouse button down. Drag the cursor down and to the right until the required range has been selected. Then release the mouse button. Now press the **Delete** key. All the cells in this range are cleared of their contents. Reverse this by **Ctrl+Z** and deselect the range by clicking on any single cell.

(2) Click on cell C4 (release the mouse button). Hold down the **Shift** key and press the **down** and **right hand arrows** until the correct range is highlighted.

Deselect the range by clicking on any single cell.

(3) Click on cell C4 (release the mouse button). Hold down the **Shift** key and click on cell D6.

Deselect the range by clicking on any single cell.

Sometimes you may want to select an entire row or column:

(4)   Say you wanted to select row 3, perhaps to change all the occurrences of £'000 to a bold font. Position your cursor over the figure 3 defining row 3 and click. All of row 3 is selected. Clicking on the **B** in the font group on the **Home** tab will make the entire row bold:

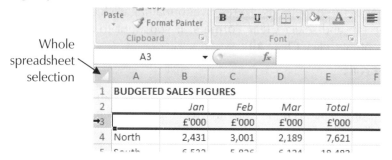

Sometimes you may want to select every cell in the worksheet, perhaps to put everything into a different font:

(5)   Click on the triangle shape at the extreme top left of the cells (indicated above). Alternatively you can select the active cells using **Ctrl + A**.

Filling a range of cells

There are a number of labour-saving shortcuts which allow you to quickly fill ranges of cells with headings (such as £'000, or month names) and with patterns of numbers. You can keep the ExcelExercise1 spreadsheet open throughout the following activities and simply open a new spreadsheet on which to experiment.

(1)   Create a new spreadsheet (**Office button>New>Create**).

(2)   Make cell B3 active and type Jan (or January) into it.

(3)   Position the cursor at the bottom right of cell B3 (you will see a black + when you are at the right spot – this is often referred to as the **fill handle**).

(4)   Hold down the mouse button and drag the cursor rightwards, until it is under row G. Release the mouse button.

The month names will automatically fill across.

(5)   Using the same technique, fill B4 to G4 with £.

(6)   Type 'Region' into cell 3A.

(7)   Type the figure 1 into cell A5 and 2 into cell A6. Select the range A5–A6 and obtain the black cross at the bottom right of cell A6. Hold down the mouse key and drag the cursor down to row 10. Release the mouse button.

The figures 1–6 will automatically fill down column A.

> **Note:** If 1 and 3 had been entered into A5 and C6, then 1, 3, 5, 7, 9, 11 would automatically appear. This does **not** work if just the figure 1 is entered into A5.

The AutoSum button Σ

We will explain how to use the AutoSum button by way of a simple example.

(1)   Clear your worksheet (**Select all>Delete**).

(2)   Enter the following figures in cells A1:B5. (**Hint.** Instead of pressing return after each figure, you can press the down or right arrow to enter the figure and to move to the next cell).

	A	B
1	400	582
2	250	478
3	359	264
4	476	16
5	97	125

(3)   Make cell B6 the active cell and select the Formulas group from the Ribbon. Click the drop-down arrow next to the **Σ AutoSum** button and select **Σ Sum**. The formula =SUM(B1:B5) will appear in the cell. Above cell B6 you will see a flashing dotted line around cells B1:B5. Accept the suggested formula by hitting Enter. 1,465 should appear in B6. Alternatively, you can simply click on the large **Σ** symbol itself, or click on the **Σ AutoSum** button in the **Editing** part of **Home** on the ribbon (see later).

(4)   Next, make cell A6 the active cell and repeat the operation for that column. The number 1,582 should appear in cell A6.

(5)   Now delete the two totals.

Copying and pasting formulae

You have already seen that formulae are extremely important in spreadsheet construction. In Excel it is very easy to define a formula once and then apply it to a wide range of cells. As it is applied to different cells the cell references in the formula are automatically updated. Say, that in the above example, you wanted to multiply together each row of figures in columns A and B and to display the answer in the equivalent rows of column C.

(1) Make C1 the active cell.

(2) Type =, then click on cell A1, then type * and click on cell B1.

(3) Press Enter

The formula =A1*B1 should be shown in the formula bar, and the amount 232,800 should be shown in C1.

(4) Make C1 the active cell and obtain the black + by positioning the cursor at the bottom right of that cell.

(5) Hold down the mouse button and drag the cursor down to row 5.

(6) Release the mouse button.

Look at the formulae in column C. You will see that the cell references change as you move down the column, updating as you move from row to row.

C3		▼	f_x	=A3*B3
	A	B	C	D
1	400	582	232800	
2	250	478	119500	
3	359	264	94776	
4	476	16	7616	
5	97	125	12125	

It is also possible to copy whole blocks of cells, with formulae being updated in a logical way.

(1) Make A1 the active cell and select the range A1:C5, for example, by dragging the cursor down and rightwards.

(2) Press **Ctrl+C** (the standard Windows Copy command) or click on the **Copy** symbol in the **Home** section of the ribbon.

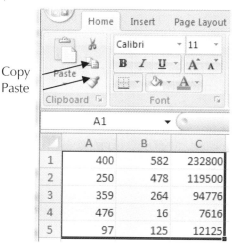

(3) Make E7 the active cell and press **Ctrl+V** or click on the paste button. E7 will become the top right cell of the copied rectangle and will hold 400.

(4) Now, look at the formulae shown in cell G7. It will show =E7*F7. So all cell references in the formulae have been updated relative to one another. This type of copying is called **relative copying**.

(5) **Delete** the range E7:G7.

Paste special

Sometimes you don't want to copy formulae and you only want to copy the displayed values. This can be done using **Paste special**.

Open the spreadsheet called Paste special example from the files available for download at www.bpp.com/aatspreadsheets.

You will see a simple inventory-type application listing quantities, prices and values. The values are obtained by formulae multiplying together prices and quantities. Say that you just want to copy the values of cells D3:D8, without the underlying formulae.

(1) Select the range D3:D8

(2) Press **Ctrl+C** or the copy icon in the **Clipboard** part of **Home** on the Ribbon

(3) **Right-click** on cell C12 to make it active, and choose **Paste Special** from the list.

(4) Check the **Values** radio button

(5) Click **OK**

The list of figures will be pasted, but if you look in the formula bar, you will see that they are just figures; there are no formulae there.

Note. If you change a quantity or price in the original table, the figures you have just pasted will not change; they have become pure numbers and do not link back to their source.

Inserting and deleting columns and rows

Often you will need to insert or delete whole rows or columns in spreadsheets. This can easily be done and sometimes formulae are correctly updated – but they should always be checked. For this exercise we will go back to using the ExcelExample1 spreadsheet.

Close the spreadsheet you have recently been working on and go back to (using the tabs across the bottom of the screen) or reopen the spreadsheet ExcelExample1.

Let us assume that we have a new region, East and that we want this to be in a row lying between North and South.

(1) Select row 5, by clicking on the 5, then click the right mouse button ('right click') and select **Insert**. You will see rows 5, 6 and 7 move down.

(2) Make B8 the active cell and you will see that the formula in the formula bar is =B4+B6+B7. If we were to put the figures for East into row 5 then those would **not** be correctly included in the total, though B5 has been updated to B6 etc.

(3) Reverse the last step (**Ctrl+Z**).

(4) Now, in cell B7 insert =SUM(B4:B6).

(5) Copy B7 across columns C7 to E7 (black cross and drag across).

(6) Check the formulae that are in cells C7 to E7 to ensure they have all been updated.

(7) Insert a whole row above row 5 (select row 5>right click>**Insert**).

(8) Inspect the formulae in row 8, the new total row.

The formulae in the total row will now be showing =SUM(B4:B7), =SUM(C4:C7), etc. In this case the new row will be included in the total. Effectively, the range over which the totals are calculated has been 'stretched'. Depending how your copy of Excel is set up, you may notice little green triangles in row 8. If so, place your cursor on one and press the exclamation symbol. The triangles are warning that you have included empty cells in your total – not a problem here, but it might have been in some cases. Don't worry if the triangles aren't showing.

(9) Finally delete row 5. Select the whole row by clicking on the 5, then right click and choose **Delete** from the menu.

The cells below Row 5 will move up and the SUM formulae are again updated.

New columns can also be added. Say that we now wanted to include April in the results.

(1) Replace the current formula in E4 with =SUM(B4:D4).

(2) Copy the formula in E4 down through columns 5, 6 and 7. Check that the correct formulae are in cells E4–E7.

(3) Select column E, by clicking on the E, then click the right mouse button ('right click') and select **Insert**. You will see column E move to the right.

(4) Inspect the formulae now in Column F, the new total column.

You will see that the formula in F7 still says = SUM(B7:D7). It has **not been updated** for the extra column.

So, if an extra row or column is inserted in the middle of a range, the formulae is updated because the new row or column probably (but not always) becomes part of the range that has to be added up.

However, if the extra row or column is added at the end of a range (or the start) the formula will not be updated to include that. That's reasonably logical as new items at the very start or end have a greater chance of being headings or something not part of the range to be included in a calculation.

So:

**Whenever columns or rows are added or deleted,
check that formulae affected remain correct.**

Tracing precedents and dependents

As spreadsheets are developed it can become difficult to be sure where figures come from and go to (despite being able to display formulae in all the cells). A useful technique is to make use of the trace precedents and trace dependents options. These are available on the **Formulas** section of the **Ribbon**.

(1) Open the Precedent example spreadsheet from the downloaded files and make cell F4 active.

(2) Choose the **Formulas** section of the Ribbon and click on **Trace Precedents** in the **Formula Auditing** group of icons.

You should see:

	A	B	C	D	E	F
1	BUDGETED SALES FIGURES					
2		Jan	Feb	Mar		Total
3		£'000	£'000	£'000		£'000
4	North	2,431	3,001	2,189		7,621
5	South	6,532	5,826	6,124		18,482
6	West	895	432	596		1,923
7	Total	9,858	9,259	8,909		28,026

Now it is very obvious that anything in column E, like April figures will not be included in the total.

(3) Click on **Remove Arrows** in the **Formula Auditing** group.

(4) Make B4 the active cell.

(5) Click on **Trace Dependents**. This will show what cells make use of this cell:

	A	B	C	D	E	F
1	BUDGETED SALES FIGURES					
2		Jan	Feb	Mar		Total
3		£'000	£'000	£'000		£'000
4	North	2,431	3,001	2,189		7,621
5	South	6,532	5,826	6,124		18,482
6	West	895	432	596		1,923
7	Total	9,858	9,259	8,909		28,026

Changing column width and height

You may occasionally find that a cell is not wide enough to display its contents. When this occurs, the cell displays a series of hashes ######. There are several ways to deal with this problem:

- Column widths can be adjusted by positioning the mouse pointer at the head of the column, directly over the little line dividing two columns. The mouse **pointer** will change to a **cross** with a double-headed arrow through it. Hold down the left mouse button and, by moving your mouse, stretch or shrink the column until it is the right width. Alternatively, you can double click when the double-headed arrow appears and the column will automatically adjust to the optimum width.

- Highlight the columns you want to adjust and choose **Home>Cells>Format>Column Width** from the menu and set the width manually. Alternatively, you can right click the highlighted column(s) and choose **Column width** from the menu.

- Highlight the columns you want to adjust and choose **Home>Format>Autofit Column Width** from the menu and set the width to fit the contents.

Setting column heights works similarly.

Dates

You can insert the current date into a cell by **Ctrl+ ;** (semicolon)

You can insert the current time by **Ctrl+Shift + ;** .

You can insert date and time by first inserting the date, release Ctrl, press space, insert the time. The date can be formatted by going to **Home>Number>Date** and choosing the format required.

Once a date is entered it is easy to produce a sequence of dates.

In a new worksheet, insert the date 1/1/2011 in cell A1.

(1) Format so as to show 01 January 2011.

(2) In A2, insert the date 8/1/2011 and format it to appear as 08 January 2011.

(3) Select cells A1 and A2.

(4) Position the cursor on the bottom right of cell A2 (a black + will appear).

(5) Hold down the mouse button and drag the mouse down to A12.

The cells should fill with dates seven days apart.

(If you see ######in a cell it means that column A is too narrow, so widen it as explained above).

Naming cells

It can be difficult to always have to refer to a cell co-ordinate, eg C12. Cell C12 might contain the VAT rate and it would be more natural (and less error prone) to refer to a name like 'VAT'.

> (1) Open the worksheet called Name example.
>
> (2) Make cell B3 the active one and right click on it.
>
> (3) Select **Name a range**.
>
> (4) Accept the offered name, 'VAT' that Excel has picked up from the neighbouring cell.
>
> (5) Highlight the range D4:D7, right click **Name a range** and accept the offered 'Net'.
>
> (6) In E4 enter =Net*(1 + VAT).
>
> (7) Copy E4 into E5:E7.
>
> You will see the formula bar refers to names. This makes understanding a spreadsheet much easier.

A list of names can be seen using the **Formulas** section of the Ribbon and clicking on **Name Manager**.

Keyboard shortcuts

Here are a few tips to quickly improve the **appearance** of your spreadsheets and speed up your work, using only the keyboard. These are all alternatives to clicking the relevant button in the **Home** section of the Ribbon.

To do any of the following to a cell or range of cells, first **select** the cell or cells and then:

(a) Press **Ctrl + B** to make the cell contents **bold**.

(b) Press **Ctrl + I** to make the cell contents *italic*.

(c) Press **Ctrl + U** to underline the cell contents.

(d) Press **Ctrl + C** to **Copy** the contents of the cells.

(e) Move the cursor and press **Ctrl + V** to **paste** the cell you just copied into the new active cell or cells.

SPREADSHEET CONSTRUCTION

All spreadsheets need to be planned and then constructed carefully. More complex spreadsheet models should include some documentation that explains how the spreadsheet is set-up and how to use it.

There can be a feeling that, because the spreadsheet carries out calculations automatically, results will be reliable. However, there can easily be errors in formulae, errors of principle and errors in assumptions. All too often, spreadsheets offer a reliable and quick way to produce nonsense.

Furthermore, it is rare for only one person to have to use or adapt a spreadsheet and proper documentation is important if other people are to be able to make efficient use of it.

The following should be kept in separate identifiable areas of the spreadsheet:

(1)   An inputs and assumptions section containing the variables (eg the amount of a loan and the interest rate, planned mark-ups, assumptions about growth rates).

(2)   A calculations section containing formulae.

(3)   The results section, showing the outcome of the calculations.

Sometimes it is convenient to combine (2) and (3).

It is also important to:

(1)   Document data sources. For example, where did the assumed growth rate come from? If you don't know that, how will you ever test the validity of that data and any results arising from it.

(2)   Explain calculation methods. This is particularly important if calculations are complex or have to be done in a specified way.

(3)   Explain the variables used in functions. Some functions require several input variables (arguments) and may not be familiar to other users.

(4)   Set out the spreadsheet clearly, using underlinings, colour, bold text etc to assist users.

In simple spreadsheets the calculations and results can often be combined. Here is an example arranged in this way (in your downloaded files this example is called 'Mortgage'):

	D9			f_x	=PMT(C3/12,C5*12,C4)					
	A	B	C	D	E	F	G	H	I	J
1	Assumptions									
2										
3	Annual interest rate		10%							
4	Amount of loan (£)		20,000							
5	Period of loan		20							
6										
7	Calculation of monthly repayments over a reducing balance mortgage lasting (years)							20		
8										
9	Monthly repayment			-£193.00		Uses the PMT function where:				
10						Monthly interest rate = annual rate/12				
11						There are 12 x Number of years mortgage payments				
12						The amount paid pays of the mortgage precisely				
13										

This example makes use of the **Cell Comment** facility (see below) in cell D9. The explanatory message appears when the cursor is over cell D9.

If we wanted to carry out the calculation for a loan of a different amount, or at a different interest rate, or for a different period, we would **overwrite the figures in the assumptions/variables section** of the spreadsheet with the new figures to calculate the revised monthly repayments.

Of course, you may not want the assumptions to be at the top left of the spreadsheet and therefore the first thing seen. However, the location of the assumptions must be made very clear to users.

Work through the example that follows.

Example: constructing a cash flow projection

You want to set up a simple six-month cash flow projection in such a way that you can use it to estimate how the **projected cash balance** figures will **change** in total when any **individual item** in the projection is **altered**. You have the following information.

(a) Sales were £45,000 per month in 20X5, falling to £42,000 in January 20X6. Thereafter they are expected to increase by 3% per month (ie February will be 3% higher than January, and so on).

(b) Debts are collected as follows.

   (i)   60% in month following sale.
   (ii) 30% in second month after sale.
   (iii) 7% in third month after sale.
   (iv) 3% remains uncollected.

(c) Purchases are equal to cost of sales, set at 65% of sales.

(d)   Overheads were £6,000 per month in 20X5, rising by 5% in 20X6.

(e)   Opening cash is an overdraft of £7,500.

(f)   Dividends: £10,000 final dividend on 20X5 profits payable in May.

(g)   Capital purchases: plant costing £18,000 will be ordered in January. 20% is payable with order, 70% on delivery in February and the final 10% in May.

Setting up the assumptions area

These assumptions have been set up in an opening spreadsheet for you.

(1)   Open the downloaded file called Cash Flow Exercise – Assumptions (**Office button>Open**).

(2)   Move the cursor over the items in columns B and G.

These columns contain the numbers or values making up the assumptions. Each of these figures has to be kept in a separate cell so that it can be separately referenced in subsequent calculations. There's no point, for example, having "Historical monthly sales 2005 (£) 45,000" all in one cell because we will have to use the amount 45,000 later.

Note the opening cash balance is -7,500 to indicate an overdraft.

We have shaded the assumptions area to make it distinct from other parts of the spreadsheet. You can change the colour of a cell, or range of cells, by selecting the cells you want to change then going to either:

(a)   **Home>Cell styles** and choosing a colour scheme, or

(b)   **Home** and then clicking the down arrow next to the paint pot icon in the toolbar and choosing a colour from there.

Headings and layout

Next we will enter the various **headings** required for the cash flow projection.

Look at the picture below. Try to recreate this in the spreadsheet you have just opened, starting with adding the heading 'The cash flow' in cell A15. Make sure you use exactly the same rows and columns as these are referred to later. The notes following the graphic may give you some help.

You want your spreadsheet to look like this:

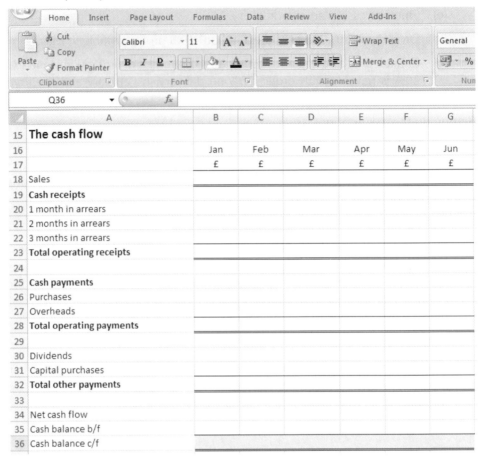

Note the following points.

(a) Column A is wider to allow longer items of text to be entered. Depending on how your copy of Excel is set up, this might happen automatically or you may have to drag the line between the A and B columns to the right.

(b) We have used a **simple style for headings**. Headings tell users what data relates to and what the spreadsheet 'does'. We have made some words **bold**, increased the size of some fonts and centralised others. This can be done by using the buttons in the **Font** group of the **Home** section of the Ribbon.

(c) When **text** is entered into a cell it is usually **left aligned** (as for example in column A). We have **centred** the headings for months and the '£' signs above each column by highlighting the cells and using the relevant buttons at the top of the screen in the **Alignment** section.

Note that if you want a heading to span across two or more columns, select the cell with the text and the cells you want the heading to appear over and click **Merge and Center** on the **Alignment** section of the **Home** tab.

(d) **Numbers** should be **right aligned** in cells. This usually happens automatically when you enter a number into a cell.

(e) We have left **spaces** in certain rows (after blocks of related items) to make the spreadsheet **easier to use and read**.

(f) Totals have been highlighted by a single line above and a double line below. This can be done by highlighting the relevant cells then going to the **Styles** group in the **Home** section of the Ribbon, clicking on the drop-down arrow and choosing the style you want, in this case '**Totals**'.

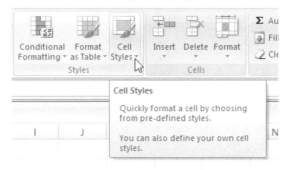

Alternatively, highlight the relevant cells, go to the **Font** area of the **Home** section and click on the drop-down arrow to access the list of borders available:

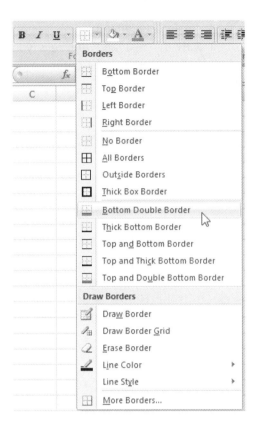

Inserting formulae

The next step is to enter the **formulae** required. For example, in cell B23 you want total operating receipts, =SUM(B20:B22). Similarly, the sales in February (cell C18) would be the sales in January increased by the assumed rate of growth of 3%.

You may be tempted to insert the formula =B18*1.03 in cell C18.

Similarly, in D18 you could put the formula = C18*1.03.

This would work, but would be poor practice. Think what would happen if you wanted to see the effect of a 5% growth rate: every formula in row 18 would have to be altered to include 1.05 rather than 1.03.

Remember what we said before: **always try to enter a variable that will be 'used' many times, such as a growth rate assumption, once only. Other cells should refer back to the cell containing that variable**.

Here, we already have the growth rate in cell B7 so the formula in cell C18 could be =B18*B7, and the formula in cell D18 could be =C18*B7. Now if we change the contents of B7 from 3% to 5% the spreadsheet is automatically updated for the new growth rate assumption.

The quick way to insert a series of formulae is to type in the initial one and then to copy across a row or down a column. You may remember that cell references are cleverly updated as you move along the row or column. This was called **relative copying**. However, that will get us into trouble here. If cell C18 contains the formula =B18*B7 and that is copied one cell to the right, into column D, the formula will become =C18*C7.

The C18 reference is correct because we are progressing along the row, one month at a time, but the C7 reference is incorrect. The location of the growth rate does not move: it is **absolute**. To prevent a cell reference being updated during the copying process put a '**$**' sign in front of the row and/or column reference.

A reference like $A1 will mean that column A is always referred to as you copy across the spreadsheet. If you were to copy down, the references would be updated to A2, A3, A4, etc.

A reference such as A$1 will mean that row 1 is always referred to as you copy down the spreadsheet. If you were to copy across, the references would be updated to B1, C1, D1, etc.

A reference like A1 will mean that cell A1 is always referred to no matter what copying of the formula is carried out.

The **function key F4** adds dollar signs to the cell reference, cycling through one, two or zero dollar signs. Press the **F4** key as you are entering the cell address.

If you haven't managed to create the outline explained above, open the spreadsheet called 'Cash flow exercise outline' (one of the spreadsheets you downloaded from www.bpp.com/aatspreadsheets).

(1) In cell B18 enter the formula =B6 (remember, it would be bad practice to enter 42,000 again: refer back to where it is first entered).

(2) In cell C18 enter the formula =B18*(1+$B7).

(3) Copy C18 across D18 to G18.

You should end up with the following figures:

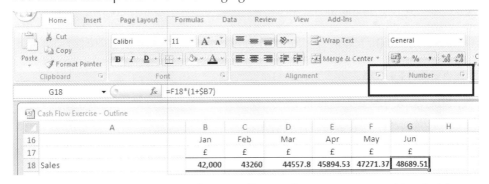

Note that the formula in G18 refers to cell F18 (the previous month's sales) but to cell B7 – the absolute address of the growth rate assumption.

The sales figure are untidy: some have comma separators between the thousands, some have one decimal place, some two. To tidy this up we will use the **Number** section of the Ribbon.

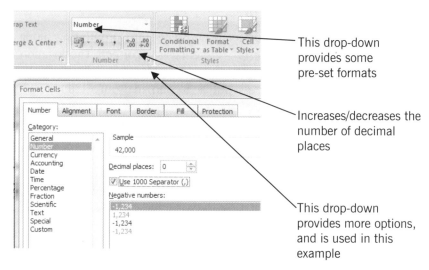

This drop-down provides some pre-set formats

Increases/decreases the number of decimal places

This drop-down provides more options, and is used in this example

---

(1)   Select the range of cells B18:G36.

(2)   Click in the small arrow just right of the word 'Number' to open the **Format Cells** window.

(3)   Select **Number**, reduce the **Decimal places** to 0 and tick the **Use 1000 Separator (,)** check-box.

You should see that all the figures in your spreadsheet are now in the same format.

Now we'll concentrate on converting the sales to cash receipts, starting with cell C20. In February we will receive 60% of the sales made in January. Once again, be on your guard against inputting the same information repeatedly: refer to other cells where possible. Here the formula =B18*B9 would work, but as we are going to copy this across other months it will be important to make the reference to cell B9 absolute. Therefore, the formula you want is =B18*$B9.

---

(1)   In cell C20 enter =B18*$B9

(2)   Copy that across cells D20 to G20

(3)   In cell D21 enter =B18*$B10

(4)   Copy that across cells E21 to G21

(5)   In cell E22 enter =B18*$B11

(6)   Copy that across cells E22 to G22

---

(7)   In cell B20 enter =B5*B9

(8)   In cell B21 enter =$B5*$B10

(9)   Copy B21 to C21

(10) In cell B22 enter =$B5*$B11

(11) Copy B22 across C22 and D22

(12) In cell B23 enter =Sum(B20:B22)

(13) Copy B23 across cells C23 to G23

(14) Format all the cells in the same way as we did for the **Sales** row

The top part of the cash flow spreadsheet should now be like this:

		Jan	Feb	Mar	Apr	May	Jun
15	**The cash flow**						
16		Jan	Feb	Mar	Apr	May	Jun
17		£	£	£	£	£	£
18	Sales	42,000	43,260	44,558	45,895	47,271	48,690
19	Cash receipts						
20	1 month in arrears	27,000	25,200	25,956	26,735	27,537	28,363
21	2 months in arrears	13,500	13,500	12,600	12,978	13,367	13,768
22	3 months in arrears	3,150	3,150	3,150	2,940	3,028	3,119
23	Total operating receipts	43,650	41,850	41,706	42,653	43,932	45,250

And the formulae behind the cell contents should be:

The cash flow

	Jan	Feb	Mar	Apr	May	Jun
	£	£	£	£	£	£
Sales	=B6	=B18*(1+$B7)	=C18*(1+$B7)	=D18*(1+$B7)	=E18*(1+$B7)	=F18*(1+$B7)
Cash receipts						
1 month in arrears	=B5*B9	=B18*$B9	=C18*$B9	=D18*$B9	=E18*$B9	=F18*$B9
2 months in arrears	=$B5*$B10	=$B5*$B10	=B18*$B10	=C18*$B10	=D18*$B10	=E18*$B10
3 months in arrears	=$B5*$B11	=$B5*$B11	=$B5*$B11	=B18*$B11	=C18*$B11	=D18*$B11
Total operating receipts	=SUM(B20:B22)	=SUM(C20:C22)	=SUM(D20:D22)	=SUM(E20:E22)	=SUM(F20:F22)	=SUM(G20:G22)

If your spreadsheet looks different from this, open the one called Cash Flow Exercise – Receipts (one of the spreadsheets you downloaded from www.bpp.com/aatspreadsheets).

Try to complete the spreadsheet, down to and including Total other payments.

You should not have to enter numbers anywhere. All your entries can be done by referencing other cells.

The spreadsheet should now look like:

15	**The cash flow**						
16		Jan	Feb	Mar	Apr	May	Jun
17		£	£	£	£	£	£
18	Sales	42,000	43,260	44,558	45,895	47,271	48,690
19	Cash receipts						
20	1 month in arrears	27,000	25,200	25,956	26,735	27,537	28,363
21	2 months in arrears	13,500	13,500	12,600	12,978	13,367	13,768
22	3 months in arrears	3,150	3,150	3,150	2,940	3,028	3,119
23	**Total operating receipts**	43,650	41,850	41,706	42,653	43,932	45,250
24							
25	Cash payments						
26	Purchases	27,300	28,119	28,963	29,831	30,726	31,648
27	Overheads	6,300	6,300	6,300	6,300	6,300	6,300
28	**Total operating payments**	33,600	34,419	35,263	36,131	37,026	37,948
29							
30	Dividends					10,000	
31	Capital purchases	3,600	12,600			1,800	
32	**Total other payments**	3,600	12,600	0	0	11,800	0

Finally, we get to the last three rows.

(1) In Cell B34 enter the formula =B23-B28-B32.

(2) Copy that across the remaining months.

(3) In cell B35 enter =G8.

(4) In cell B36 enter =B34+B35.

(5) Copy that across the remaining months.

(6) In cell C35 (the brought forward balance for February) enter =B36 (the carried forward balance from January.

(7) Copy that across the remaining months.

The finished spreadsheet should look like this:

	A	B	C	D	E	F	G	H
1	**Cash flow projection: six months January - June 20X6**							
2								
3	Assumptions/variables							
4								
5	Historical monthly sales 20X5 (£)	45,000		Purchases = cost of sales.			65%	of sales
6	Projected sales Jan 20X6 (£)	42,000		Monthly overheads 20X5 (£)			6,000	
7	Monthly sales growth (2/X6 onwards)	3%		Rise in monthly overheads 20X6			5%	
8	Collection of debts:			Opening cash balance (O/d)			-7,500	
9	Month following sales	60%		Dividends (payable May 20X6, £)			10,000	
10	2nd month following sales	30%		Capital expenditure			18,000	
11	3rd month following sales	7%		Payable January			20%	
12	Uncollected	3%		Payable February			70%	
13				Payable May			10%	
14								
15	**The cash flow**							
16		Jan	Feb	Mar	Apr	May	Jun	
17		£	£	£	£	£	£	
18	Sales	42,000	43,260	44,558	45,895	47,271	48,690	
19	Cash receipts							
20	1 month in arrears	27,000	25,200	25,956	26,735	27,537	28,363	
21	2 months in arrears	13,500	13,500	12,600	12,978	13,367	13,768	
22	3 months in arrears	3,150	3,150	3,150	2,940	3,028	3,119	
23	Total operating receipts	43,650	41,850	41,706	42,653	43,932	45,250	
24								
25	Cash payments							
26	Purchases	27,300	28,119	28,963	29,831	30,726	31,648	
27	Overheads	6,300	6,300	6,300	6,300	6,300	6,300	
28	Total operating payments	33,600	34,419	35,263	36,131	37,026	37,948	
29								
30	Dividends					10,000		
31	Capital purchases	3,600	12,600			1,800		
32	Total other payments	3,600	12,600	0	0	11,800	0	
33								
34	Net cash flow	6,450	-5,169	6,443	6,521	-4,894	7,302	
35	Cash balance b/f	-7,500	-1,050	-6,219	224	6,746	1,852	
36	Cash balance c/f	-1,050	-6,219	224	6,746	1,852	9,154	

If your figures are different, you will find the above spreadsheet Cash Flow Exercise – Finished within the files downloaded from www.bpp.com/aatspreadsheets.

Tidy the spreadsheet up

The presentation is reasonable as we have taken care of it as we have developed the spreadsheet. This is good practice.

However, you may like to change **negative numbers** from being displayed with a **minus sign** to being displayed in **brackets**. This will require a special format. Depending on what your copy of Excel has been used for previously, that format may already exist, or you may have to create it.

To look for or create the cell format:

> (1) Highlight the Cash Flow range B16:G36.
>
> (2) Click on the small arrow next to **Number** on the ribbon and choose **Custom** from the bottom of the category list.
>
> (3) Scroll down the **Type** list looking for a Type with the pattern: #,##0;(#,##0).
>
> (4) The #,## indicates that a comma is to be used as the 000 separator.
>
> (5) The 0 indicates no decimal places.
>
> (6) #,##0 before the semicolon indicates the format of positive numbers.
>
> (7) (#,##0) after the semi-colon indicates the format of negative numbers.
>
> (8) If a suitable format is not found in the list, then create one by:
>
> (9) Clicking on the format 0 (just after general).
>
> (10) Type #,##0;(#,##0) or, even better, #,##0;[red](#,##0).
>
> (11) Click OK.
>
> If you use the second suggestion, negative numbers will be in brackets **and** coloured red.

Other cell formatting options available from the same **Number** section of the Ribbon include formatting as a particular currency or as a percentage.

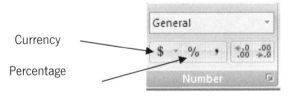

Take some time to play with these formatting options. Remember, you can always undo any action by pressing **Ctrl + Z**.

Add more information or explanation

It would be useful to know the basis or source of assumption and calculation methods. A simple way in which this can be documented is to use the Cell Comment facility.

Right click on cell B7 and choose **Insert comment** option for the list.

A box appears into which you can type your comment, such as:

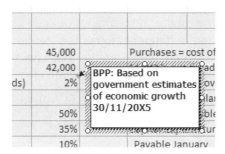

Press **Enter**.

A small red triangle is now visible at the top right off the cell indicating that it contains a comment. The comment appears if the cursor is placed on the cell.

Example: commission calculations

The following four telesales people each earn a basic salary of £14,000 pa. They also earn a commission of 2% of sales. The following spreadsheet has been created to process their commission and total earnings. Give an appropriate formula for each of the following cells.

(a) Cell D4
(b) Cell E6
(c) Cell D9
(d) Cell E9

	A	B	C	D	E
1	Sales team salaries and commissions - 200X				
2	Name	Sales	Salary	Commission	Total earnings
3		£	£	£	£
4	Northington	284,000	14,000	5,680	19,680
5	Souther	193,000	14,000	3,860	17,860
6	Weston	12,000	14,000	240	14,240
7	Easterman	152,000	14,000	3,040	17,040
8					
9	Total	641,000	56,000	12,820	68,820
10					
11					
12	Variables				
13	Basic Salary	14,000			
14	Commission rate	0.02			
15					

Solution

Possible formulae are:

    (a)   =B4*B14

    (b)   =C6+D6

    (c)   =SUM(D4:D7)

    (d)   There are a number of possibilities here, depending on whether you set the cell as the total of the earnings of each salesman (cells E4 to E7) or as the total of the different elements of remuneration (cells C9 and D9). Even better, would be a formula that checked that both calculations gave the same answer. A suitable formula for this purpose would be:

        =IF(SUM(E4:E7)=SUM(C9:D9),SUM(E4:E7),"ERROR")

We explain this formula after the next example, don't worry about it at the moment!

Example: actual sales compared with budget sales

A business often compares its results against budgets or targets. It is useful to express differences or **variations as a percentage of the original budget**, for example sales may be 10% higher than predicted.

Continuing the telesales example, a spreadsheet could be set up as follows showing differences between actual sales and target sales, and expressing the difference as a percentage of target sales.

	A	B	C	D	E
1	Sales team comparison of actual against budget sales				
2	Name	Sales (Budget)	Sales (Actual)	Difference	% of budget
3		£	£	£	£
4	Northington	275,000	284,000	9,000	3.27
5	Souther	200,000	193,000	(7,000)	(3.50)
6	Weston	10,000	12,000	2,000	20.00
7	Easterman	153,000	152,000	(1,000)	(0.65)
8					
9	Total	638,000	641,000	3,000	0.47
10					

Give a suitable formula for each of the following cells.

    (a)   Cell D4

    (b)   Cell E6

    (c)   Cell E9

Try this for yourself, before looking at the solution.

Solution

(a)　=C4 – B4

(b)　=(D6/B6)*100

(c)　=(D9/B9)*100. Note that in (c) you **cannot simply add up the individual percentage differences**, as the percentages are based on different quantities

FORMULAE WITH CONDITIONS

Suppose the employing company in the above example awards a bonus to people who exceed their target by more than £1,000. The spreadsheet could work out who is entitled to the bonus.

To do this we would enter the appropriate formula in cells F4 to F7. For salesperson Easterman, we would enter the following in cell F7:

　　=IF(D4>1000,"BONUS"," ")

We will now explain this **IF** function.

IF statements follow the following structure (or 'syntax').

　　=IF(logical_test, value_if_true, value_if_false)

The logical_test is any value or expression that can be evaluated to Yes or No. For example, D4>1000 is a logical expression; if the value in cell D4 is over 1,000, the expression evaluates to Yes. Otherwise, the expression evaluates to No.

Value_if_true is the value that is returned if the answer to the logical_test is Yes. For example, if the answer to D4>1000 is Yes, and the value_if_true is the text string "BONUS", then the cell containing the IF function will display the text "BONUS".

Value_if_false is the value that is returned if the answer to the logical_test is No. For example, if the value_if_false is two sets of quote marks "" this means display a blank cell if the answer to the logical test is No. So in our example, if D4 is not over 1,000, then the cell containing the IF function will display a blank cell.

Note the following symbols which can be used in formulae with conditions:

　　<　　less than

　　<=　　less than or equal to

　　=　　equal to

　　>=　　greater than or equal to

　　>　　greater than

　　<>　　not equal to

Care is required to ensure **brackets** and **commas** are entered in the right places. If, when you try out this kind of formula, you get an error message, it may well be a simple mistake, such as leaving a comma out.

Using the IF function

A company offers a discount of 5% to customers who order more than £10,000 worth of goods. A spreadsheet showing what customers will pay may look like:

	C8			f_x	=IF(B8>C3, B8*C4,0)	
	A	B	C	D	E	F
1	Sales discount					
2						
3	Discount hurdle		10,000			
4	Discount rate		5%			
5						
6	Customer	Sales	Discount	Net price		
7		£	£	£		
8	John	12,000	600	11,400		
9	Margaret	9,000	0	9,000		
10	William	8,000	0	8,000		
11	Julie	20,000	1000	19,000		
12						
13						
14						
15						

The formula in cell C8 is as shown: =**IF**(B8>C3, B8*C4, 0). This means, if the value in B8 is greater than £10,000 multiply it by the contents of C4, ie 5%, otherwise the discount will be zero. Cell D8 will calculate the amount net of discount, using the formula: =B8−C8. The same conditional formula with the cell references changed will be found in cells C9, C10 and C11.

Here is another example for you to try.

Open the spreadsheet called Exam Results (one of the spreadsheets downloaded from www.bpp.com/aatspreadsheets).

There are ten candidates listed together with their marks.

The pass mark has been set at 50%.

See if you can complete column C rows 6–15 so that it shows PASS if the candidate scores 50 or above, and FAIL if the candidate scores less than 50.

Once it's set up and working correctly, change the pass mark in cell B3 to 60 and ensure that the PASS/FAIL indications reflect the change.

The formulae you need will be based on the one for cell C6.

C6		fx =IF(B6>=B3, "PASS","FAIL")

Book3

	A	B	C	D	E	F
1	**Exam results**					
2						
3	Pass mark	50				
4						
5	Candidate	Mark	Pass/fail			
6	Alf	51	PASS			
7	Beth	56	PASS			
8	Charles	82	PASS			
9	David	42	FAIL			
10	Edwina	68	PASS			
11	Frances	36	FAIL			
12	Gary	75	PASS			
13	Hugh	53	PASS			
14	Iris	72	PASS			
15	John	34	FAIL			

Conditional formatting

In addition to the condition determining whether PASS or FAIL appear, you can also conditionally format cell contents – for example, by altering the colour of a cell to highlight problems. This can be done by accessing the **Conditional Formatting** option in the **Styles** section of the **Home** tab of the Ribbon.

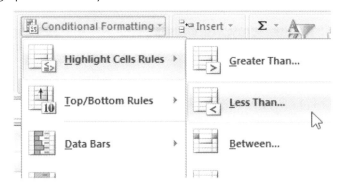

The marks which are less than the value in B3 have been highlighted by making the cell background red and the text white, as illustrated below:

	A	B	C
1	**Exam results**		
2			
3	Pass mark	50	
4			
5	Candidate	Mark	Pass/fail
6	Alf	51	PASS
7	Beth	56	PASS
8	Charles	82	PASS
9	David	42	FAIL
10	Edwina	68	PASS
11	Frances	36	FAIL
12	Gary	75	PASS
13	Hugh	53	PASS
14	Iris	72	PASS
15	John	34	FAIL

To produce the above result:

Change the pass mark back to 50% if it is still at 60%.

Highlight the numbers in column B.

Click **Conditional formatting>Highlight cell rules>Less than**. You will see there are two white entry boxes.

Click on cell B3. This will be entered automatically into the first box.

Then click on the down arrow next to the second entry box. Click on **Custom format>Fill** and choose the red box. This changes the colour of the cell.

Then click on **Font** and click the down arrow next to 'Automatic', under **Colour** and choose the white box.

Click **OK**.

CHARTS AND GRAPHS

Charts and graphs are useful and powerful ways of communicating trends and relative sizes of numerical data. Excel makes the production of charts relatively easy through the use of the chart wizard.

We will use the Sales discount spreadsheet (one of the spreadsheets downloaded from www.bpp.com/aatspreadsheets) to generate a number of different charts.

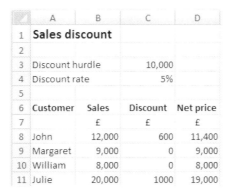

	A	B	C	D
1	**Sales discount**			
2				
3	Discount hurdle		10,000	
4	Discount rate		5%	
5				
6	Customer	Sales	Discount	Net price
7		£	£	£
8	John	12,000	600	11,400
9	Margaret	9,000	0	9,000
10	William	8,000	0	8,000
11	Julie	20,000	1000	19,000

First, we will generate a simple pie chart showing the total sales figure, before discounts.

A simple pie chart

(1) Open the Sales discount spreadsheet.

(2) Place your cursor on the word 'Customer', hold down the mouse button and drag the cursor downwards until you have selected the four names and four sales figures.

(3) Select the **Insert** section from the Ribbon, then **Pie/3-D pie**.

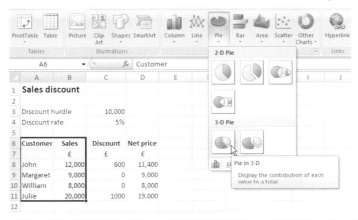

This will generate a pie chart that looks like this:

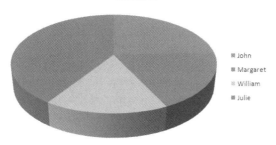

Sales £

You will see that it already has a title, 'Sales £'. To make any changes to this, double click the area where the title appears, then enter additional text or delete text you do not want. Below we have added 'for 2006' and brackets around the pound sign.

Sales for 20X6 (£)

Changing the chart type

If you decide that a different chart may be more suitable for presenting your data you can easily change the chart type.

(1)   Click on your chart. The **Chart Tools** options should become available at the top of the window.

(2)   Click **Design>Change Chart Type**.

(3)   From here, pick some charts from the following chart types to see what they produce: **Bar**, **Bubble**, **Doughnut** and **Line**. For example the doughnut chart will produce something like this:

Sales for 20X6 (£)

Bar charts

A pie chart is good for showing relative sizes of elements making up a total. However, sometimes you may want to be able to compare how two series of data are moving: sales and gross profit for example. In this case, bar charts (or line charts) are more suitable. Excel makes a distinction between bar charts that show vertical bars and those that show horizontal bars. When the data is shown vertically Excel refers to the chart as a 'column' chart whereas if the data is shown horizontally it is a 'bar' chart.

We are going to create a column chart showing the Sales and Net Price figure from the data on the Sales Discount spreadsheet.

> (1) Delete your chart by clicking on its outer most frame and pressing the **Delete** key.
>
> (2) Place the cursor on the word 'Customer' and drag the cursor down until all four names have been selected.
>
> (3) Hold down the Ctrl button and select B6:B11. Still holding the Ctrl button down, select D6:D11.
>
> (4) Release the mouse button and Ctrl key.
>
> (5) On the Ribbon, choose **Insert>Column>3D Clustered Column**.

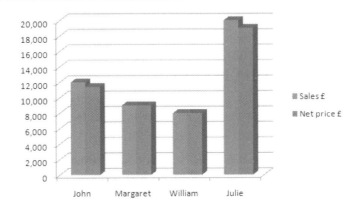

This time there is no automatic chart title so we will need to add one.

> Click on the chart. At the top of the window you will see **Chart Tools** appear:
>
>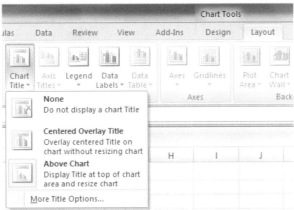
>
> From the **Labels** section, choose **Layout>Chart Title>Above Chart**.
>
> Type in "Sales and Net Prices for 20X6 (£)".

To the right of the chart you will see a description for each column. This is called a Legend. You can move the legend by clicking on the **Legend** button.

Sales and Net Prices for 20X6 (£)

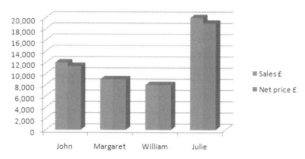

You should also label the horizontal axis and the vertical axis.

(1) To label the horizontal axis, click **Layout>Axis Titles>Primary Horizontal Axis>Title below axis** (make sure you are clicked on the chart to see the **Chart Tools** tabs)

(2) The words 'Axis Title' appear at the bottom of the chart. Click on this, then press **Ctrl + A** to select all the words and type in your axis title, in this case 'Customer'.

(3) To label the other axis, this time choose **Primary Vertical Axis**. You have a choice of directions for your text. Choose **Horizontal Title** and type a pound sign.

Note that if you are typing words for the vertical axis title the best option is usually **Rotated Title**. Try experimenting with that now.

Sales and Net Prices for 20X6 (£)

Formatting existing charts

Even after your chart is 'finished' you can change it in a variety of ways.

(a) You can **resize it** simply by selecting it and dragging out one of its corners.

(b) You can change the scale by dragging out the top, base or sides. To do so, hover your cursor over the four dots in the middle of the relevant top, base or side until your cursor turns into a **double ended arrow**. Click and it will turn into a large cross, then drag with the mouse button still held down.

(c) You can change **each element** by **clicking** on it then selecting from the options available on the various **Chart tools** tabs.

(d) You can also select any item of **text** and alter the wording, size or font, or change the **colours** used using the buttons on the **Font** section of the Home part of the ribbon. For example, practice increasing and decreasing the size of the font by clicking on the text you wish to change, then experimenting with the two different sized capital A buttons:

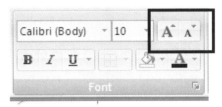

(e) There is also a variety of colour schemes available from the Ribbon, under **Chart Tools>Design>Chart Styles**.

PRINTING, LINKING AND EMBEDDING

Printing spreadsheets

The print options for your spreadsheet may be accessed by selecting **Office button** and **Print>Print**, or pressing **Ctrl + P**. Printing large spreadsheets without checking the print and layout settings will often result in printouts spread messily over several pages.

It is a good idea to at least opt for **Print Preview** to see what your printout will look like before printing.

A better option is to control what prints more precisely. This can be done from the **Page Layout** section of the Ribbon.

This allows you to, for example, print out selected areas only, include/exclude grid-lines and the column and row headings, alter the orientation of the page and so on.

Open the spreadsheet we saw earlier called Cash Flow Exercise – Finished.

Assume that we only want to print out the cash flow without the table at the top showing the assumptions. We want to show the gridlines but not the A, B, C... or 1, 2, 3... that head up columns and rows.

(1) Select the range A15:G36

(2) Choose **Page Layout>Print Area>Set Print Area** from the Ribbon

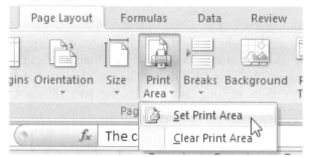

(3) Check the **Print Gridlines** box in **Page Layout>Sheet** options

(4) Choose **Office Button>Print>Print Preview**

The printout will stretch over two pages, with just the June figures on the second page. This is clearly unsatisfactory.

Close the **Print Preview** window.

Looking back at the Cash Flow spreadsheet, you will see a double dotted line around the print area selected, but between May and June there is a single dotted line indicating where Excel automatically made the unfortunate page break.

The easiest way to solve this problem is:

Choose **Page Layout>Width>1 page** in the **Scale to fit** section of **Page Layout**.

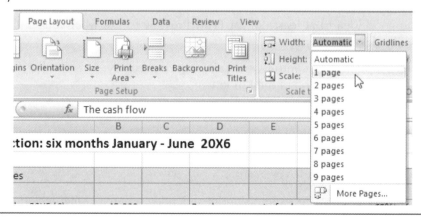

You will see the page break line disappears and a Print Preview will show the selected areas all on one page.

At this point you can check for obvious layout and formatting errors.

Spelling

Before you print, it is wise to check your work for spelling mistakes. To do this click the **Review** tab and select **Spelling**. If you have made any spelling errors Excel will offer alternative **Suggestions** which you can accept by clicking **Change** or ignore by clicking **Ignore** (**Once** or **All**).

If the word is in fact correct (for example, terminology that Excel does not recognise) you can add it to Excel's dictionary by clicking **Add to Dictionary**.

Preparing your spreadsheet for printing: Page set-up

The **Page Setup** area of the **Page Layout** tab on the Ribbon also allows you to specify certain other details that affect how your spreadsheet looks when it prints out.

From here you can set the size of the **Margins** (the white spaces that print around the spreadsheet) and choose whether to print the spreadsheet in landscape **Orientation** (ie wider than tall) rather than the default portrait **Orientation** (taller than wide).

Imagine you are printing out a spreadsheet that will cover several pages. It is important that certain information is present on each page. For example:

- The spreadsheet title
- The page number and total pages
- The author
- The row and column headings

This can be done by accessing the **Page Setup** options, by clicking on the little arrow in the bottom right corner of the section, or by clicking on the **Print Titles** icon.

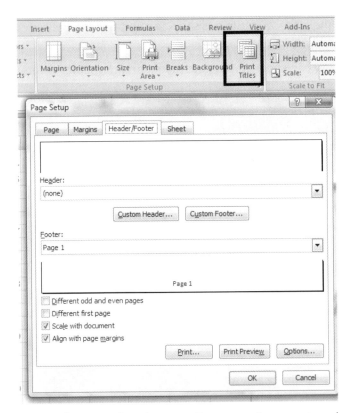

Headers appear at the top of each page. For example, a custom header could be:

Author   Budget for 2012   Date printed

Footers appear at the bottom of each page, for example:

Page   File name

The **Sheet** tab allows you to specify the rows and columns to be repeated on each page. For example, you might want to repeat the months across the top of each page and the type of income down the left of each page.

> We have provided a demonstration spreadsheet in the downloaded files, Print practice. Open it and try the following:
>
> > Insert a **Header**: Author name, Title (Budget 2012) Date printed
> >
> > Insert a **Footer**: Page number, File name
>
> Click **Page setup** (or **Print Titles**)>**Header/Footer**> **Custom Header** and **Custom Footer**.
>
> Ensure that the headings in column A are repeated on the second page.

Use this spreadsheet to experiment with page breaks (**Breaks**) and the other remaining options in the **Page Setup** area.

Printing formulae

Occasionally, perhaps for documentation or checking, you might want the spreadsheet formulae to be printed out instead of the calculated results of the formula. To do this:

(1)   Display the formulae on the screen by pressing **Ctrl + `** .

(2)   Set the area you want to be printed: **Page Layout>Print Area>Set Area**

(3)   Check what the printout will look like **Office button>Print>Print preview**

(4)   Adjust as necessary and print out when happy with the display

Printing charts

Charts can be printed either with or without the data on the worksheet.

To print only the chart simply click on it and then press **Ctrl + P**. As always it is wise to **Print Preview** first.

If you also want to print the worksheet data, click away from the chart into any cell. Use **Print Preview** to make sure that the chart is the right size and is in the right position. Then press **Ctrl + P**.

USING SPREADSHEETS WITH WORD PROCESSING SOFTWARE

There may be a situation where you wish to incorporate the contents of all or part of a spreadsheet into a **word processed report**. There are a number of options available to achieve this.

(a)   The simplest, but least flexible option, is to **print out** the spreadsheet and interleave the page or pages at the appropriate point in your word processed document.

(b)   A neater option, if you are just including a small table, is to select and **copy** the relevant cells from the spreadsheet to the computer's clipboard by selecting the cells and Pressing **Ctrl+C** (or using the **Copy** button on the Home section of the Ribbon). Then switch to the word processing document, and **Paste** them in (for example, by using **Ctrl+V**) at the appropriate point. The pasted material is now completely separate from its source spreadsheet. If the spreadsheet is changed, the copied and pasted material will not change, and you have to go through the copy/paste procedure again to update the report.

(c) Office packages, such as Microsoft Office, allow you to **link** spreadsheets and word processing files.

For example, a new, blank spreadsheet can be 'embedded' in a document by selecting **Insert>Object** then, from within the **Create New** tab, selecting **Microsoft Office Excel Worksheet**. The spreadsheet is then available to be worked upon, allowing the easy manipulation of numbers using all the facilities of the spreadsheet package. Clicking outside the spreadsheet will result in the spreadsheet being inserted into the document.

The contents of an existing spreadsheet may be inserted into a Word document by choosing **Insert>Object** and then activating the **Create from File** tab. Then click the **Browse** button and locate the spreadsheet file. Highlight the file, then click **Insert**, ensure you click the box next to the **Link to File** option, and then **OK**. You may then need to move and resize the object, by dragging its borders, to fit your document.

Provided Automatic update has been activated in the Word file, the linked object will be updated every time you open the file that contains the object or any time the linked object changes while the file is open.

---

(1) Open the downloaded spreadsheet called Linking Experiment.

(2) Save this to a location you will remember, for example, the desktop:

Office button>Save as>Desktop>Linking experiment

(3) Keep Excel open, but now open Word and create a new document.

(4) In Word click **Insert>Object>Create from File** and browse to find the Linking Experiment file you just saved.

(5) Ensure the '**Link to File**' box is checked.

(6) Click **OK**.

You will see the Linking Experiment appear in the Word document.

(7) Keep the Word file open, but switch back to the Excel and the open Linking Experiment spreadsheet.

(8) Change the top figure to 15 (the total will change to 43).

(9) Look again at the Word file and you will see that it has also been changed in line with the linked spreadsheet.

You can close the file without saving as you won't need them again.

Importing data to Excel

You may wish to include data in a spreadsheet that comes from, say, a Microsoft Word document, a PowerPoint Presentation or another spreadsheet.

The easiest way to do this is select the text you wish to include, click the **Home** tab and click **Copy** (or press **Ctrl + C**).
Open the spreadsheet that you wish to use the data in if it is not already open and click the **Paste** button (or press **Ctrl + V**).

CHAPTER OVERVIEW

- A **spreadsheet** is basically an electronic piece of paper divided into **rows** and **columns**. The intersection of a row and a column is known as a **cell**.

- Essential basic **skills** include how to **move around** within a spreadsheet, how to **enter** and **edit** data, how to **fill** cells, how to **insert** and **delete** columns and rows and how to improve the basic **layout** and **appearance** of a spreadsheet.

- **Relative** cell references (eg B3) change when you copy formulae to other locations or move data from one place to another. **Absolute** cell references (eg B3) stay the same.

- A wide range of **formulae** and functions are available within Excel. We looked at the use of conditional formulae that use an **IF** statement.

- A spreadsheet should be given a **title** which clearly defines its purpose. The contents of rows and columns should also be clearly **labelled**. **Formatting** should be used to make the data in the spreadsheet easy to read and interpret.

- **Numbers** can be **formatted** in several ways, for instance with commas, as percentages, as currency or with a certain number of decimal places.

- Excel includes the facility to produce a range of charts and graphs. The **Chart Wizard** provides a tool to simplify the process of chart construction.

- Spreadsheets can be **linked** to, and exchange data with, **word processing documents** – and *vice versa*.

- Spreadsheets can be used in a variety of accounting contexts. You should practise using spreadsheets, **hands-on experience** is the key to spreadsheet proficiency.

TEST YOUR LEARNING

Test 1

List three types of cell contents.

Test 2

What do the F5 and F2 keys do in Excel?

Test 3

What technique can you use to insert a logical series of data such as 1, 2 .... 10, or Jan, Feb, March etc?

Test 4

How do you display formulae instead of the results of formulae in a spreadsheet?

Test 5

List five possible changes that may improve the appearance of a spreadsheet.

Test 6

What is the syntax (pattern) of an IF function in Excel?

Test 7

The following spreadsheet shows sales of two products, the Ego and the Id, for the period July to September.

	A	B	C	D	E
1	Sigmund Ltd				
2	Sales analysis - quarter 3, 2010				
3		July	August	September	Total
4	Ego	3,000	4,000	2,000	9,000
5	Id	2,000	1,500	4,000	7,500
6	Total	5,000	5,500	6,000	16,500

Devise a suitable formula for each of the following cells.

(a)   Cell B6
(b)   Cell E5
(c)   Cell E6

Test 8

The following spreadsheet shows sales, exclusive of VAT, the VAT amounts and the VAT inclusive amounts. There is a strong possibility that the VAT rate of 17.5% will change soon so it is important to construct the spreadsheet so that it can easily be adapted.

	A	B	C	D
1	Taxable Supplies Ltd		Vat rate	0.175
2				
3		January	February	March
4	Product A	5,000	4,000	3,000
5	Product B	2,000	1,500	4,000
6	Product C	7,000	5,700	4,000
7	Product D	2,000	3,000	1,000
8	Product E	1,000	2,400	6,000
9	Total net	17,000	16,600	18,000
10	VAT	2,975	2,905	3,150
11	Total gross	19,975	19,505	21,150

Suggest suitable formulae for cells:

(a)   B9
(b)   C10
(c)   D11

chapter 2:
MORE ADVANCED SPREADSHEET TECHNIQUES (EXCEL 2007)

---

chapter coverage 📖

In this chapter we explore some of the more advanced aspects of spreadsheets using Excel 2007.

This chapter covers:

✍ The importance of regularly saving and backing up spreadsheets.

✍ Controlling access to spreadsheets, including making spreadsheets available for sharing.

✍ Checking the validity of data when entering it into a spreadsheet.

✍ Working with multiple worksheets that refer to each other.

✍ Sophisticated data handling including sorting, filtering, pivot tables and look-up tables.

✍ Statistical tools and functions that help in analysing data.

✍ Using combination charts to compare two sets of unrelated data on the same chart.

✍ Error detection and prevention.

CONTROLS, SECURITY AND SHARING

Back-ups, passwords and cell protection

There are facilities available in spreadsheet packages which can be used as controls – to prevent unauthorised or accidental amendment or deletion of all or part of a spreadsheet. There are also facilities available for hiding data, and for preventing (or alerting) users about incorrect data.

Saving files and backing up

(a) **Save**. When working on a spreadsheet, save your file regularly, as often as every ten minutes, using **Office button>Save** or pressing **Ctrl + S**. This will prevent too much work being lost in the event of a system crash.

Save files in the appropriate **folder** so that they are easy to locate. If you need to save the file to a new folder, choose the '**New folder**' option after clicking **Office button>Save**. Where this option is located depends on the operating system you are using. For example, in Windows 7, you simply click the **New folder** button (see below).

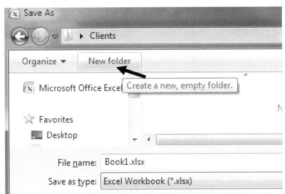

Give the folder a suitable name (for example, the name of the client you are working on or following your employer's standard naming practice).

(b) **Save as**. A simple **save** overwrites the existing file. If you use **Save as** then you can give the file a different name, preserving previous versions. For example Save as "Budget Edition 1", "Budget Edition 2", "Budget Edition 3". This is much safer than simply relying on the most recent version – which might be beyond fixing!

(c) **Back-ups**. Because data and the computers or storage devices on which it is stored can easily be lost or destroyed, it is vital to take regular copies or back-ups. If the data is lost, the back-up copy can be used to **restore** the data up to the time the back-up was taken. Spreadsheet files should be included in standard backup procedures, for example the daily back-up routine.

The back-ups could be held on a separate external hard drive, or perhaps a USB memory stick, and should stored away from the original data, in case there is a fire or other disaster at the organisation's premises. Alternatively the back-ups can be saved to a network location. Some back-ups are now stored on the Internet.

(d) **AutoRecover**. Excel has a built-in feature that saves copies of all open Excel files at a fixed time interval. The files can be restored if Excel closes unexpectedly, such as during a power failure.

Turn on the AutoRecover feature by clicking **Office button>Excel Options>Save**.

The default time between saves is every 10 minutes. To change this, click the **Save AutoRecover info every** check box and enter any number of minutes between 1 and 120.

In the **AutoRecover file location** box, you can type the path and the folder name of the location in which you want to keep the AutoRecover files.

Protection

(a) **Cell protection/cell locking**. This prevents the user from inadvertently changing cells that should not be changed. There are two ways of specifying which cells should be protected.

(i) All cells are locked except those specifically unlocked.

This method is useful when you want most cells to be locked. When protection is implemented, all cells are locked unless they have previously been excluded from the protection process. You will also see here a similar mechanism for hiding data.

> (1) Once again, open the spreadsheet Cash Flow Exercise–Finished.
>
> (2) Highlight the range B5:B12. This contains some of the assumptions on which the cash flow forecast is based and this is the only range of cells that we want to be unlocked and available for alteration.
>
> (3) In the **Home** section of the Ribbon, click on the small arrow beside **Fonts** and then choose **Protection**.

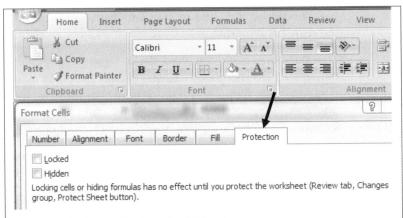

Locking cells or hiding formulas has no effect until you protect the worksheet (Review tab, Changes group, Protect Sheet button).

(4)   Untick the **Locked** and **Hidden** boxes.

(5)   Click on **OK**.

(6)   Now go to the **Review** group on the Ribbon.

(7)   Click on **Protect Sheet**.

(8)   Don't enter a password when prompted, simply click **OK**.

Now investigate what you can change on the spreadsheet. You should find that only cells B5:B12 can be changed. If you try to change anything else a message comes up telling you that the cell is protected.

Click on **Unprotect Sheet** to make every cell accessible to change again.

(ii)   Most are unlocked, except those specified as being locked.

This method is useful if only a few cells have to be locked.

(1)   Open the spreadsheet Sales discount.

(2)   Assume that we want to lock only the 10,000 in cell C3 and the 5% figure in cell C4.

(3)   Select the whole spreadsheet and, as we did above, click on the small arrow beside **Fonts**. Then choose **Protection** and untick the **Locked** and **Hidden** boxes. The cells can still be changed if you do not do this step.

(4)   Select the range of cells C3:C4.

(5)   In the **Home** section of the Ribbon go to the **Cells** group and click on **Format**.

(6)   Click on **Lock Cell**.

(7)   Click on **Protect Sheet** from the same **Format** menu. The cells remain editable if you do not do this step.

You are offered the chance to enter a password.

Now you will be prevented from changing just those two cells.

(b) **Passwords**. There are two levels of password.

(i) All access to the spreadsheet can be protected and the spreadsheet encrypted. This can be done by:

> (1) **Office button>Prepare>Encrypt Document**.
>
> (2) You are then asked to enter and verify a password. Heed the warning: if you forget the password, there's no likelihood of recovery of the spreadsheet.
>
> (3) To remove the password protection use:
>
> (4) **Office button>Prepare>Encrypt Document**
>
> (5) Then delete the asterisks in the password box and click OK.

(ii) The spreadsheet can be password protected from amendment but can be seen without a password. This can be done as follows:

> (1) At the bottom of the **Save As** dialogue click **Tools**.
>
> (2) Choose **General Options**.
>
> (3) You can choose here again a Password to open.
>
> (4) In the Password to modify box type a password, then retype it to confirm and click **OK**.
>
> (5) Click **Save**.

Now, if you close the file and re-open it, you will be asked for a password to get full access, or without the password you can open it in read-only mode so that it can be seen but not changed.

Sharing workbooks

It is possible to share a workbook with colleagues so that the same file can be viewed by more than one person at a time. This can be done in a number of ways.

Send as an attachment

One way to share a spreadsheet with colleagues is to send it as an attachment in an email. If your computer is set up with a mail client such as Microsoft Outlook you can click **Office Button>Send>E-mail** to quickly send the spreadsheet you are working on as an attachment.

Alternatively you can first draft the email and attach the spreadsheet using your email program's options and the Windows Explorer menu.

However, if each recipient of the email makes changes to the document, this will lead to the existence of a number of different versions of the same document, and a potential loss of version control. This is not, therefore, a recommended method of sharing spreadsheets.

Save to a shared network server

Another way to make a spreadsheet available to colleagues is to save it in a place on the network server that is also accessible to them. Anyone with access to that particular location will be able to open the file but, if more than one person tries to open the file, only the first person will be able to make changes to it. Anyone else subsequently opening the file will only be able to open a 'Read Only' version of it, so they will be able to view the contents but not make any changes.

This method prevents loss of version control but is not particularly useful if other people wish to make changes at the same time.

Share workbook method

A more practical method is to use the inbuilt sharing function in Excel. This allows different people to open and make changes to the same document at the same time, and for these changes to be tracked.

Click the **Review** tab on the Ribbon. In the **Changes** section click the **Share Workbook** button. Click the **Editing** tab and select **Allow changes by more than one user at the same time**. From this tab you can also see who has the document open.

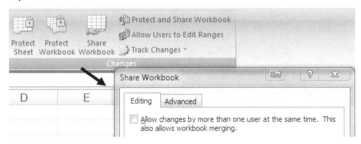

Other settings are available from the **Advanced** tab such as choosing how long to keep the change history for, how frequently to update changes and what to do if users make conflicting changes.

To stop any tracked changes from being lost click **Protect and Share Workbook** and click **Sharing with tracked changes**. This option also allows you to set a password so only those with the password can make changes.

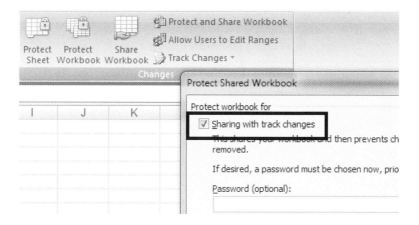

Data validation

Sometimes only a specific type or range of data is valid for a certain cell or cells. For example, if inputting hours worked in a week from a time sheet it could be known that no one should have worked more than 60 hours. It is possible to test data as it is input and to either prevent input completely or simply warn that the input value looks odd. This is known as 'data validation' or 'data restriction'.

In this simple spreadsheet, C2 holds the only formula; A2 and B2 are cells into which data will be entered, but we want the data to conform to certain rules:

Hours <= 60. If greater than 60, a warning is to be issued.

Rate/hr >=8 and <=20. Data outside that range should be rejected.

(1) Set up a new spreadsheet with the above data and make A2 the active cell. Go to **Data>Data Validation** (in **Data Tools** section).

(2) Under the **Data Validation Settings** tab, **Allow Decimal**, select less than or equal to from the drop-down list and enter 60 as the Maximum.

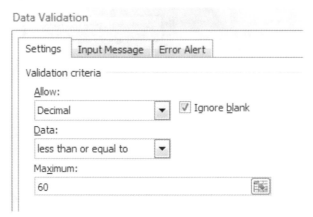

(3) Under the **Input Message** tab enter 'Warning' as the title and 'Hours expected to be less than 60' as the input message.

(4) Under the **Error Alert** tab change the **Style** to Warning, enter 'Attention' as the title and 'Check hours: look too large' as the **Error message**.

(5) Click OK.

(6) Now try to enter 70 into A2. You will first see an information message explaining what data is expected, then a warning message and the option to continue.

(7) Now try to set up cell B2 with appropriate messages and to prevent any value outside the range 8–20 from being entered at all.

THREE DIMENSIONAL (MULTI-SHEET) SPREADSHEETS

Background

In early spreadsheet packages, a spreadsheet file consisted of a single worksheet. As mentioned earlier, Excel provides the option of multi-sheet spreadsheets, consisting of a series of related sheets.

For example, suppose you were producing a profit forecast for two regions, and a combined forecast for the total of the regions. This situation would be suited to using separate worksheets for each region and another for the total. This approach is sometimes referred to as working in **three dimensions**, as you are able to flip between different sheets stacked in front or behind each other. Cells in one sheet may **refer** to cells in another sheet. So, in our example, the formulae in the cells in the total sheet would refer to the cells in the other sheets.

Excel has a series of 'tabs', one for each worksheet at the bottom of the spreadsheet.

How many worksheets?

Excel can be set up so that it always opens a fresh file with a certain number of worksheets ready and waiting for you. Click on **Office button>Excel Options>Popular**, and set the number **'Include this many sheets'** option to the number you would like each new workbook to contain (sheets may be added or deleted later).

If you subsequently want to insert more sheets you just click on the new sheet tab.

By default sheets are called Sheet 1, Sheet 2 etc. However, these may be changed. To rename a sheet in Excel, right click on its index tab and choose the **Rename** option. You can drag the sheets into different orders by clicking on the tab, holding down the mouse button and dragging a sheet to its new position.

Pasting from one sheet to another

When building a spreadsheet that will contain a number of worksheets with identical structure, users often set up one sheet, then copy that sheet and amend its contents.

To copy a worksheet in Excel, from within the worksheet you wish to copy, select **Home>Cells>Format>Move or Copy Sheet** (or right click the worksheet tab and select **Move or Copy Sheet**) and tick the **Create a copy** box.

A 'Total' sheet would use the same structure, but would contain formulae totalling the individual sheets.

Linking sheets with formulae

Formulae on one sheet may refer to data held on another sheet. The links within such a formula may be established using the following steps.

Step 1   In the cell that you want to refer to a cell from another sheet, type =.

Step 2   Click on the index tab for the sheet containing the cell you want to refer to and select the cell in question.

Step 3   Press **Enter**.

---

(1) Open the spreadsheet called 3D spreadsheet example.

This consists of three worksheets. The Branch A and Branch B sheets hold simple trading and profit and loss accounts. There are both numbers and formulae in those sheets. The Company sheet contains only headings, but is set out in the same pattern as the two branch sheets.

We want to combine the Branch figures onto the Company sheet.

(2) On the company sheet, make D2 the active cell

(3) Enter =

(4) Click on Branch A and click on D2

(5) Enter +

(6) Click on Branch B and click on D2

(7) Press **Enter**

You will see that the formula ='Branch A'!D2+'Branch B'!D2 is now in cell D2 of the Company sheet and that the number displayed is 500,000, the sum of the sales in each branch.

In the company sheet, copy D2 (**Ctrl+C**) and paste (**Ctrl+V**) to D3, D4, C6, C7, C8, and D9 to complete the profit and loss account.

The company sheet will now look like this:

	A	B	C	D
	3D spreadsheet example			
1	Company		£	£
2	Sales			500,000
3	Cost of sales			270,000
4	Gross profit			230,000
5	Expenses:			
6	Selling and distribution		70,000	
7	Administration		45,000	
8				115,000
9	Net profit			115,000
10				

This is arithmetically correct, but needs lines to format it correctly.

Use the border facility in **Home>Font** to insert appropriate single and double lines (borders) in the cells:

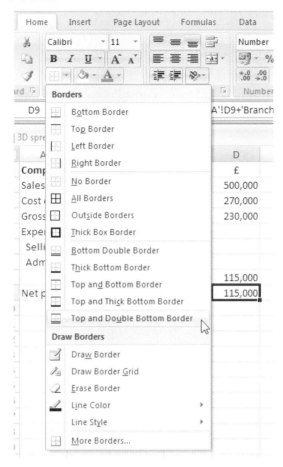

The final consolidated results should look like:

	A	B	C	D
1	Company		£	£
2	Sales			500,000
3	Cost of sales			270,000
4	Gross profit			230,000
5	Expenses:			
6	Selling and distribution		70,000	
7	Administration		45,000	
8				115,000
9	Net profit			115,000

Note that if you change any figures in Branch A or Branch B, the figures will also change on the company spreadsheet.

Uses for multi-sheet spreadsheets

There are a wide range of situations suited to the multi-sheet approach. A variety of possible uses follow.

(a) A spreadsheet could use one sheet for variables, a second for calculations, and a third for outputs.

(b) To enable quick and easy **consolidation** of similar sets of data, for example the financial results of two subsidiaries or the budgets of two departments.

(c) To provide different views of the same data. For instance, you could have one sheet of data sorted into product code order and another sorted into product name order.

DATA MANIPULATION

Data manipulation refers to a number of techniques available in Excel for summarising, analysing, sorting and presenting data.

Simple data manipulation

A database can be viewed simply as a collection of data. There is a simple 'database' related to inventory, called Stockman Ltd within the files downloaded from www.bpp.com/aatspreadsheets. **Open it now**.

There are a number of features worth pointing out in this spreadsheet before we start data manipulation.

(1) Each row from 4–15 holds an inventory record.

(2) Column G makes use of the **IF** function to determine if the inventory needs to be reordered (when quantity < reorder level).

(3) In row 2, the spreadsheet uses automatic word wrap within some cells. This can improve presentation if there are long descriptions. To use word wrap, select the cells you want it to apply to then click the **Wrap Text** icon in the **Alignment** section of the **Home** tab. The height of the cells needs to be increased to accommodate more than one line of text. To do this, select the whole row then double click on the line between the row numbers 2 and 3, or instead, select **AutoFit Row Height** as shown below.

The data is currently arranged in part number order.

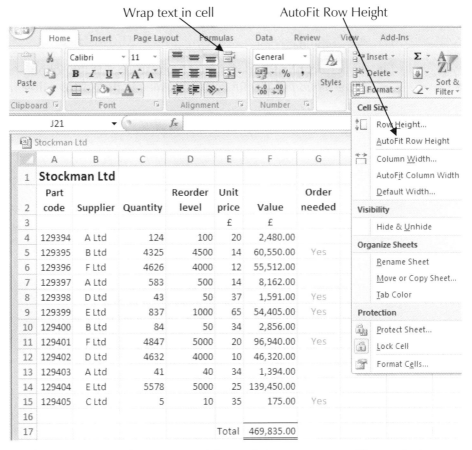

Wrap text in cell   AutoFit Row Height

	Part code	Supplier	Quantity	Reorder level	Unit price £	Value £	Order needed
1	Stockman Ltd						
4	129394	A Ltd	124	100	20	2,480.00	
5	129395	B Ltd	4325	4500	14	60,550.00	Yes
6	129396	F Ltd	4626	4000	12	55,512.00	
7	129397	A Ltd	583	500	14	8,162.00	
8	129398	D Ltd	43	50	37	1,591.00	Yes
9	129399	E Ltd	837	1000	65	54,405.00	Yes
10	129400	B Ltd	84	50	34	2,856.00	
11	129401	F Ltd	4847	5000	20	96,940.00	Yes
12	129402	D Ltd	4632	4000	10	46,320.00	
13	129403	A Ltd	41	40	34	1,394.00	
14	129404	E Ltd	5578	5000	25	139,450.00	
15	129405	C Ltd	5	10	35	175.00	Yes
16							
17					Total	469,835.00	

The horizontal rows are records: one record for each inventory type. The vertical columns are attributes (qualities) relating to each record.

Sorting the data

Let's say that we want to sort the data into descending value order.

---

(1) Select the data range A4:G15

(2) At the right-hand side of the **Home** section of the Ribbon (and in the **Data** section of the Ribbon) you will see the **Sort & Filter** drop-down menu

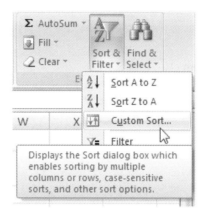

(3) Choose **Custom Sort**

(4) Sort by Column F, largest to smallest.

(5) Click **OK**.

You will see that the data has been sorted by value.

If you now **Sort by** Supplier (**Order A–Z**) you will have the data arranged by supplier, and within that by value.

Filtering the data

Filtering data allows you to select and display just some of it in the table. This is useful if the table consists of many records but you only wish to view some of them.

Sort the data back into Part code order.

Let's say we just want to find inventory records relating to suppliers B and C.

Select **Filter** from the **Sort & Filter** drop-down menu.

Click on the drop-down arrow that has appeared at the top of the Supplier column.

Deselect (ie click on the box to remove the tick) **Select All**, then select B and C.

Click on **OK**.

Only the records relating to suppliers B and C are visible and these can be manipulated (eg sorted) as an independent subset of the whole table.

Note that the other records are still there and are included in the total value figure. It's simply that they have been hidden for presentation.

You will also see a little funnel symbol at the top of the Supplier column informing that there is filtering in place.

Make all the records visible again by removing the filter:

(1) Drop-down arrow in the Supplier column

(2) Select **Select All**

(3) Click on **OK**

(4) Sort the data back into Part code order if it's not already in that order

To get rid of the little filter arrows, click on the funnel symbol in the **Sort & Filter** area of the Ribbon to disengage it.

Find and replace

Let's now say that that Supplier A Ltd has been taken over and that its name has changed to Acorn plc.

---

(1) Make all the records visible again by removing the filter if you haven't already.

(2) Click on the **Find & Select** symbol and select **Find** (or press **Ctrl + F**)

(3) Enter A Ltd in the **Find what**: box

(4) Click on the **Replace** tab and enter Acorn Plc in the **Replace with**: box

(5) Click on **Replace All**

Note. You could instead click on **Find & Select>Replace** (or press **Ctrl + H**) as a shortcut.

You should see that all occurrences of A Ltd have been replaced by Acorn plc.

If no range is specified before this step then the whole spreadsheet would be affected. If a range is specified, the search and replace occurs only within that range.

Σ AutoSum

You have already used Σ AutoSum as a way of specifying a range of data to add up. However, the Σ AutoSum drop-down list also contains other useful functions such as:

- **Average**
- **Count numbers**
- **Maximum**
- **Minimum**

Still using the Stockman Ltd spreadsheet:

> (1) Select cells E4..E15
>
> (2) From the **Σ AutoSum** drop-down list (you can find this on both the **Home** and **Formulas** tabs of the Ribbon) select **Max**
>
> You will see 65 appear in cell E16 (just below the last unit price). The formula in that cell is =MAX(E4:E15).
>
> Try some of the other **Σ AutoSum** functions.

The results given by **Σ AutoSum** are always just under a column of data, or immediately to the right of a row of data.

If you want the results to appear in a different cell, you have to type the appropriate formula into that cell. For example, typing =MAX(E4:E15) into cell A20 will show the maximum unit price of the inventory in cell A20.

Formatting data as a table

You can format data within a spreadsheet as a table. This provides you with another way to present and manipulate data.

Creating a table

First we will create a table and then we'll look at what we can do with it.

> (1) **Open** the Tables example spreadsheet from the downloaded files. This uses almost the same data as in the previous exercise, so should look familiar to you.
>
> (2) Select the cells that contain the data (A3 to G15).
>
> (3) On the **Home** tab of the Ribbon select **Format as Table** from the **Styles** section.
>
> (4) A gallery of styles will appear, so choose one of the formats (any one will do). Check that the correct data for the table is selected in the white box and tick the box **My table has headers**.
>
> (5) Click **OK**.
>
> (6) Your table should now look something like this, depending on which format you chose:
>
>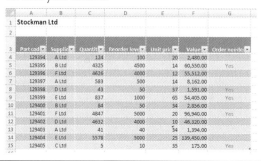

You will notice that there are **Sort & Filter** drop down arrows at the top of each column in the header row. This is just one of the benefits of formatting data as a table: automatic **Sort & Filter**.

Other benefits of formatting data as a table

Other benefits include:

(a) **Easy row and column selection**

Move the cursor to the top of the header row of the table and it will change to a thick pointing arrow. When you click, just the data in that column will be selected (and not the empty cells below the data). You can select data rows in a similar way.

The whole table can be selected by hovering near the table's top left corner until the arrow becomes thick and starts pointing towards the bottom right hand corner.

(b) **Visible header row when scrolling**

When you scroll down past the bottom of the table the column letters become the table's column names so long as you have clicked anywhere inside the table before starting scrolling.

	Part code	Supplier	Quantity	Reorder level	Unit price	Value	Order needed
4	129394	A Ltd	124	100	20	2,480.00	
5	129395	B Ltd	4325	4500	14	60,550.00	Yes
6	129396	F Ltd	4626	4000	12	55,512.00	
7	129397	A Ltd	583	500	14	8,162.00	
8	129398	D Ltd	43	50	37	1,591.00	Yes
9	129399	E Ltd	837	1000	65	54,405.00	Yes
10	129400	B Ltd	84	50	34	2,856.00	
11	129401	F Ltd	4847	5000	20	96,940.00	Yes
12	129402	D Ltd	4632	4000	10	46,320.00	
13	129403	A Ltd	41	40	34	1,394.00	
14	129404	E Ltd	5578	5000	25	139,450.00	
15	129405	C Ltd	5	10	35	175.00	Yes
16							

(c) **Automatic table expansion**

Type anything into any of the cells around the table and the table will automatically grow to include your new data. The formatting of the table will automatically adjust (this will also happen if you insert or delete a row or column).

(d) **Automatic formula copying**

If you enter a formula in a cell around the table and click **Enter**, the column will automatically resize to fit the formula, which is automatically copied down to fill the entire column alongside your data.

Changing the design of the table

You can change how the table looks by clicking anywhere in the table and selecting **Design** tab from the **Table Tools** toolbar.

From here there are a number of **Table Style Options** that you can play around with, such as formatting a **First Column** or **Last Column**, adding a **Total Row** and changing the **Table Style**.

You can also choose to give your table a name so that any formula you enter which uses the figures from the table will refer to that table by its name.

So, for example, type 'Parts' into the **Table Name** box:

Now any formula entered in the column next to the table will refer to the table by name. Try it!

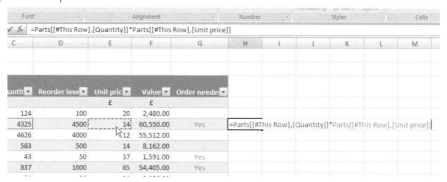

Table tools

From the **Design** tab you can also:

- Choose to **Remove Duplicates**, which, as the name suggests, removes duplicate data from the table,

- **Summarize with PivotTable** (see below), and

- Remove the table formatting completely by selecting **Convert to Range**. You may then wish to clear the formatting. You can easily do this by clicking **Clear** on the **Editing** section of the **Home** tab and choosing **Clear formats**.

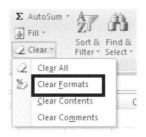

Pivot tables

Pivot tables are a very powerful way of analysing data. Look at the following simple example relating to sales by a music company.

🔲 Pivot table example

	A	B	C
1	**Sales data**		
2			
3	**Customer**	**Source**	**Amount spent (£)**
4	Bill	CDs	50
5	Chris	Vinyl	10
6	Sandra	Merchandise	30
7	Graham	CDs	45
8	Chris	Merchandise	20
9	Chris	Vinyl	10
10	Chris	CDs	10
11	Caroline	Merchandise	30
12	Graham	Tickets	75
13	Fred	Vinyl	30
14	Bill	CDs	20
15	Graham	CDs	60
16	Chris	Vinyl	10
17	Sandra	Tickets	50
18	Bill	Tickets	26
19	Caroline	Vinyl	24
20			
21		Total	£500

The information has simply been listed and totalled on the spreadsheet. It would be useful to be able to show:

- Sales per customer
- Sales by source

Ideally, we would like to produce a table which displays sales by both source and by customer: this type of table is called a pivot table.

(1) Open the spreadsheet file called Pivot table example which contains the above data.

(2) Select the range A4:C19

(3) On the Ribbon, select **Insert>Pivot Table**

(4) Select the **Existing Worksheet** radio button on the **Create PivotTable** option window

(5) Enter E4 as the location

(6) Click **OK**. The PivotTable Field List window opens

(7) Check Customer, Source, Amount spent (£)

(8) You will see that Customer and Source go by default into Row labels. The resulting table is quite useful, but not quite what we wanted.

Therefore:

(9) Drag Customer from Row Labels to Column Labels

The pivot table is now transformed into the two-dimensional table we want.

(10) Tidy it up a little by selecting F5 to L5 and right justifying these names by clicking on the appropriate Home>Alignment button on the Ribbon.

Note the two drop down arrows on the pivot table that allow filtering of the data.

Sum of Amount spent (£)	Column Labels						
Row Labels	Bill	Caroline	Chris	Fred	Graham	Sandra	Grand Total
CDs	70		10		105		185
Merchandise		30	20			30	80
Tickets	26				75	50	151
Vinyl		24	30	30			84
Grand Total	96	54	60	30	180	80	500

If you had difficulty with this, the spreadsheet called 'Pivot table result Excel 2007' is available within the downloaded files.

Experiment with different settings. Clicking on the pivot table will bring up the **PivotTable Field List** window again if it has disappeared.

Note that if the original data is altered, the pivot table does *not* change until you right-click on it and select **Refresh** from the list of options.

Look-up tables

The Look-up function allows you to find and use data that is held in a table. Here is a simple example:

	A	B	C	D	E	F	G	H	I
1	Salesman Ltd								
2	Part code	VATcode	Unit price		VAT rate	17.500%			
3			£						
4	129394	1	20.00						
5	129395	1	14.00		Invoice				
6	129396	0	12.00						
7	129397	0	14.00						
8	129398	1	37.00		Part code	Quantity	Unit price	VAT	£
9	129399	0	65.00		129396	10	12.00	0	120.00
10	129400	1	34.00				Net		120.00
11	129401	0	20.00				VAT		0.00
12	129402	1	10.00				Total		120.00
13	129403	0	34.00						
14	129404	0	25.00						
15	129405	1	35.00						
16									

On the left is a price list. If a part has a VAT code of 1, then VAT will be charged at the rate as set in cell F2; if the VAT code is 0, then no VAT is chargeable.

To create this invoice, you would look down the part numbers column until you found 129396. You would then read across to find the unit price and VAT code and, together with the quantity sold, you could create the invoice.

This process has been automated in the spreadsheet Salesman Ltd that is on your CD.

> (1) Open the Spreadsheet called Salesman Ltd.
>
> (2) Click on cell G9 to reveal the use of the VLOOKUP function.

Cell G9 holds the formula =VLOOKUP(E9,A4:C15,3, FALSE)

This means: look for the value held in cell E9, in the first row of the range A4:C15, and return the value in the third column of the range: it will return the price relating to the part number. FALSE (at the end of the statement) asks it to find an exact match so if a non-existent part code is entered in E9 you will get an error message (#N/A).

Similarly, cell H9 holds the formula =VLOOKUP(E9,A4:C15,2) and will return the VAT code relating to the part number.

Cell I11 holds a conditional (IF) function that will calculate VAT if the VAT code is 1 and insert 0 if the VAT code is 0.

Note that some cells have been formatted to show two decimal places and some to show no decimal places. Cell F2 is formatted as a percentage and, because

VAT might need to be changed, VAT is held in only one location with other cells referring to it.

Try out different part codes and quantities in the invoice.

CHANGES IN ASSUMPTIONS (WHAT-IF? ANALYSIS)

We referred earlier to the need to design a spreadsheet so that **changes in assumptions** do **not** require **major changes** to the spreadsheet. In our Cash Flow Exercise workbook we set up two separate areas of the spreadsheet, one for assumptions and opening balances and one for the calculations and results. We could simply change the values in the assumptions cells to see how any changes in assumptions affect the results.

However, if we have more than one value to change, or we want to see the result of a number of different assumption changes we can use one of the three 'What-if' functions.

Data tables

A **data table** is a way to see different results by altering an input cell in a formula. You can create one- or two-variable data tables.

Let's try creating a one-variable data table.

(1) Open the earlier spreadsheet Mortgage which used the PMT formula

(2) Enter 1% to 10% in cells E8 to L8 as shown below. You will need to increase the width of cell J8.

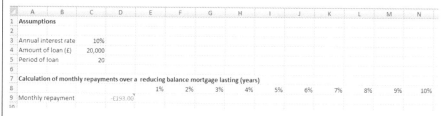

(3) Select cells D8 to M9

(4) **Click Data>What-If Analysis>Data Table**

(5) Here you want your data table to fill in the values in row 9, based on the results if the value in cell C3 were to change to a different percentage, so choose the **Row input cell** box and enter C3

You should get the following results:

	1%	2%	3%	4%	5%	6%	7%	8%	9%	10%
-£193.00	-91.9789	-101.177	-110.92	-121.196	-131.991	-143.286	-155.06	-167.288	-179.945	-193.004

The table would look better if the numbers were formatted in the same way as the first result in cell D9. An easy way to copy a format from one cell to another is to click on the cell whose format you wish to copy then click the **Format Painter** button on the **Clipboard** area of the **Home** tab and then click on the cells you wish to format.

Try it now. Click on cell D9, then click the **Format Painter** button. Now select cells E9:M9. You should see:

	1%	2%	3%	4%	5%	6%	7%	8%	9%	10%
-£193.00	-£91.98	-£101.18	-£110.92	-£121.20	-£131.99	-£143.29	-£155.06	-£167.29	-£179.95	-£193.00

Note. If you double click the **Format Painter** button you can then click any number of cells afterwards to apply that same format. To stop the **Format Painter**, simply click **Esc** (Escape).

Now let's try a two-variable data table using the same workbook. This time we want to see the result if both the interest rate and the number of years of the loan change.

(1) Rename the worksheet you have been working on to 'One variable'. Now select Sheet2 (or insert a new worksheet if necessary) and rename it 'Two variable'. This is the sheet that we will now use.

(2) **Copy** the data on the One variable worksheet (**Ctrl + C**) and paste (**Ctrl + V**) into the new worksheet.

(3) Select cells E8 to M8 and move them up down by one cell (ie to E9 to M9). You can do this by hovering over the selected cells until a cross with four arrow heads appears, then click and drag to cell E9. Alternatively, **Cut (Ctrl + X)** and then **Paste (Ctrl + V)** to cell E9.

(4) In cells D10 to D14 insert different loan periods. We have used 10, 15, 20, 25 and 30 years as shown below:

-£193.00	1%	2%	3%	4%	5%	6%	7%	8%	9%	10%
10										
15										
20										
25										
30										

(5) Select cells D9 to M14

(6) **Click Data > What-If Analysis > Data Table**

(7) Here you want the data table to fill in the values based on the results if the value in cell C3 were to change to a different percentage (as shown in row 9) and also if the loan period in C5 changes (as shown in column D). So, choose the **Row input cell** box and enter C3 and then select the **Column input cell** box and enter C5.

You should get the following results:

-£193.00	1%	2%	3%	4%	5%	6%	7%	8%	9%	10%
10	-£175.21	-£184.03	-£193.12	-£202.49	-£212.13	-£222.04	-£232.22	-£242.66	-£253.35	-£268.27
15	-£119.70	-£128.70	-£138.12	-£147.94	-£158.16	-£168.77	-£179.77	-£191.13	-£202.85	-£219.31
20	-£91.98	-£101.18	-£110.92	-£121.20	-£131.99	-£143.29	-£155.06	-£167.29	-£179.95	-£197.76
25	-£75.37	-£84.77	-£94.84	-£105.57	-£116.92	-£128.86	-£141.36	-£154.36	-£167.84	-£186.80
30	-£64.33	-£73.92	-£84.32	-£95.48	-£107.36	-£119.91	-£133.06	-£146.75	-£160.92	-£180.82

The cells should already be formatted correctly.

Finally practice saving the file as 'Mortgage – Data tables' in a new folder on your computer using **Office button>Save as**. Choose an appropriate name for the folder – it's your choice! You can also open the file of that name from your CD.

Scenarios

The Scenarios function allows you to change information in cells that affect the final totals of a formula and to prepare instant reports showing the results of all scenarios together.

Using the spreadsheet Cash Flow Exercise – Finished, we will show the result of changing the following assumptions:

(a) Sales growth will only be 2% per month.

(b) Negotiations with suppliers and gains in productivity have resulted in cost of sales being reduced to 62% of sales.

(c) The effects of a recession have changed the cash collection profile so that receipts in any month are 50% of prior month sales, 35% of the previous month and 10% of the month before that, with bad debt experience rising to 5%.

You could simply change the relevant cells in the spreadsheet to reflect these changes in assumptions. However, we are going to use the Scenario Manager function.

(1) Select the **Data** tab and from the **Data Tools** section click **What-If Analysis>Scenario Manager**

(2) Click **Add** and give the scenario an appropriate name, for example 'Original cash flow'

(3) Press the tab button or click in the **Changing cells** box and, based on the information we used above, select the cells with the changing data, ignoring the change to the opening bank balance. To select cells that are not next to each other, use the Ctrl button. You should **Ctrl click** on cells B7, B9, B10, B11 and G5.

(4) Click **OK**

(5) You are now asked for **Scenario Values**. This will show the values currently in the cells specified, which are our original figures so click **OK**

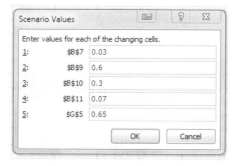

(6) We now need to enter our new values. Click **Add** and type a new **Name** (for example Cash Flow 2). The **Changing Cells** box will already contain the correct cells.

(7) Click **OK**.

(8) In the **Scenario Values** boxes change the values as follows and click **OK**

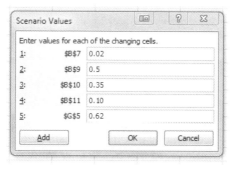

(9) Your second scenario should be highlighted. Now if you click on **Show** the figures in your assumptions table should automatically change and you can view the results.

	A	B	C	D	E	F	G	H
1	Cash flow projection: six months January - June 20X6							
2								
3	Assumptions/variables							
4								
5	Historical monthly sales 20X5 (£)	45,000		Purchases = cost of sales.			62%	of sales
6	Projected sales Jan 20X6 (£)	42,000		Monthly overheads 20X5 (£)			6,000	
7	Monthly sales growth (20X6 onwards	2%		Rise in monthly overheads 20X			5%	
8	Collection of debts:			Opening cash balance (O/d)			-7,500	
9	Month following sales	50%		Dividends (payable May 20X6,			10,000	
10	2nd month following sales	35%		Capital expenditure			18,000	
11	3rd month following sales	10%		Payable January			20%	
12	Uncollected	3%		Payable February			70%	
13				Payable May			10%	
14								
15	The cash flow							
16		Jan	Feb	Mar	Apr	May	Jun	
17		£	£	£	£	£	£	
18	Sales	42,000	42,840	43,697	44,571	45,462	46,371	
19	Cash receipts							
20	1 month in arrears	22,500	21,000	21,420	21,848	22,285	22,731	
21	2 months in arrears	15,750	15,750	14,700	14,994	15,294	15,600	
22	3 months in arrears	4,500	4,500	4,500	4,200	4,284	4,370	
23	Total operating receipts	42,750	41,250	40,620	41,042	41,863	42,701	
24								
25	Cash payments							
26	Purchases	26,040	26,561	27,092	27,634	28,187	28,750	
27	Overheads	6,300	6,300	6,300	6,300	6,300	6,300	
28	Total operating payments	32,340	32,861	33,392	33,934	34,487	35,050	
29								
30	Dividends					10,000		
31	Capital purchases	3,600	12,600			1,800		
32	Total other payments	3,600	12,600	0	0	11,800	0	
33								
34	Net cash flow	6,810	(4,211)	7,228	7,109	(4,423)	7,650	
35	Cash balance b/f	(7,500)	(690)	(4,901)	2,327	9,436	5,012	
36	Cash balance c/f	(690)	(4,901)	2,327	9,436	5,012	12,663	
37								
38								

(10) Click back on your original cash flow scenario and then click **Show** and the numbers will change back

Note. You may need to make your screen smaller to view the whole sheet at the same time. You can do this by clicking **View** on the Ribbon, then in the **Zoom** section clicking on **Zoom** and choosing a smaller percentage. 75% should be perfect.

2: More advanced spreadsheet techniques (Excel 2007)

You can also easily and quickly create a report from the scenarios.

> (1) Click **Data>What-If Analysis>Scenario Manager**
>
> (2) Click the **Summary** button
>
> (3) In the **Result cells** box choose the cells to go into the report, ie the ones you want to see the results of. As we are interested in the cash flow select cells B34:G34

This creates a separate **Scenario Summary** worksheet. Open the Cash Flow Exercise – What-if spreadsheet if you do not see the following report.

Scenario Summary			
	Current Values:	Original cash flow	Cash flow 2
Changing Cells:			
B7	3%	3%	2%
B9	60%	60%	50%
B10	30%	30%	35%
B11	7%	7%	10%
G5	65%	65%	62%
Result Cells:			
B34	6,450	6,450	6,810
C34	(5,169)	(5,169)	(4,211)
D34	6,443	6,443	7,228
E34	6,521	6,521	7,109
F34	(4,894)	(4,894)	(4,423)
G34	7,302	7,302	7,650

Notes: Current Values column represents values of changing cells at time Scenario Summary Report was created. Changing cells for each scenario are highlighted in gray.

Goal seek

What if you already know the result you want from a formula but not the value the formula itself needs to calculate the result? In this case you should use the **Goal Seek** function, which is located in the **Data Tools** section of the **Data** tab on the Ribbon.

Open the original Mortgage spreadsheet from the downloaded files. Let's assume that we have enough income to pay a monthly mortgage payment of £300 and want to know how many years it will take to pay off the mortgage.

(1) Copy the data on Sheet1 and paste it to Sheet2

(2) Click **Data>What-If Analysis>Goal Seek**

(3) **Set cell** to D9, as this is the figure we know and enter -300 in the **To value** box (make sure that you enter a negative figure to match the figure already in D9)

(4) Enter C5 in the **By changing cell** box, as this is the figure we are looking for

(5) Click **OK**

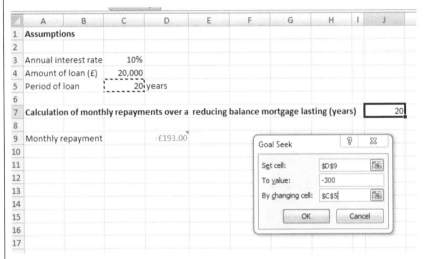

Goal seek will find the solution, 8.14 years, and insert it in cell C5.

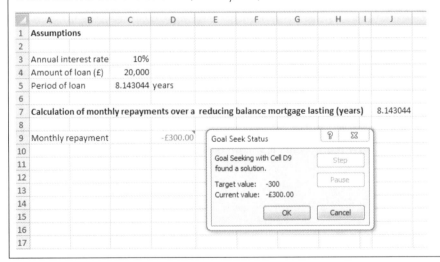

STATISTICAL FUNCTIONS

Linear regression/trends

Excel contains powerful statistical tools for the analysis of information such as how costs vary with production volumes and how sales vary through the year.

Look at the following example of costs and volume:

Month	Volume	Costs £
1	1,000	8,500
2	1,200	9,600
3	1,800	14,000
4	900	7,000
5	2,000	16,000
6	400	5,000

It is clear that at higher production volumes costs are higher, but it would be useful to find a relationship between these variables so that we could predict what costs might be if production were forecast at, say, 1,500 units.

The first investigation we could perform is simply to draw a graph of costs against volume. Volume is the independent variable (it causes the costs) so should run on the horizontal (x) axis.

Open the spreadsheet called Cost_volume and draw a scatter graph showing cost against volume, with appropriate labels and legends.

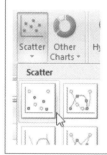

(1)   Select the range B1:C7.

(2)   Using Insert/Chart from the Ribbon, choose the top left Scatter graph type).

It should look something like the following:

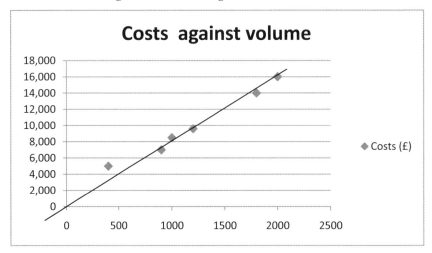

The straight line through the points has been manually drawn here to show that there's clearly a good association between volume and cost because the points do not miss the line by much, but we want to analyse this properly so that we can make a fairly good prediction of costs at output of say 1,500 units.

Lines of the sort above have a general equation of the type:

$$y = mx + b$$

Here **y** = Total costs
     x = Volume
     m = Variable cost per unit (the slope of the line)
     b = The fixed cost (where the line crosses the y axis: the cost even at zero volume)

Excel provides two easy ways of finding the figures we need for predicting values.

Find the trend:

(1)   On the same spreadsheet (Cost_volume), enter 1,500 in cell B9

(2)   Now click on cell C9

(3)   From the Ribbon choose **Formulas>More Functions>Statistical**

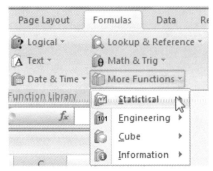

(4) Scroll down the list until you get to **TREND** and choose that

(5) For **Known_y's** select the range C2:C7

(6) For **Known_x's** select the range B2:B7

(These ranges are the raw material which the calculation uses)

For **New_x's**, enter B9, the volume for which we want the costs to be predicted.

The number 12,003 should appear in cell C9. That is the predicted cost for output of 1,500 units – in line with the graph. In practice, we would use 12,000. Altering the value in B9 will produce the corresponding predicted cost.

A second way of analysing this data will allow us to find the variable and fixed costs of the units (**m** and **b** in the equation $y = mx + b$).

(1) To find **m** use the statistical function **LINEST** and assign the **Known_y's** and **Known_x's** as before. You should get the answer 7.01, the variable cost per unit.

(2) To find the intersection, **b**, use the statistical function **INTERCEPT**. You should get the answer 1,486.

Note: These can be used to predict the costs of 1,500 units by saying:

Total costs = $1,486 + 7.01 \times 1,500 = 12,001$, more or less as before.

The spreadsheet called Cost_volume finished contains the graph, and the three statistical functions just described.

Moving averages

Look at this data

Year	Quarter	Time series	Sales $'000
2006	1	1	989.0
	2	2	990.0
	3	3	994.0
	4	4	1,015.0
2007	1	5	1,030.0
	2	6	1,042.5
	3	7	1,036.0
	4	8	1,056.5
2008	1	9	1,071.0
	2	10	1,083.5
	3	11	1,079.5
	4	12	1,099.5
2009	1	13	1,115.5
	2	14	1,127.5
	3	15	1,123.5
	4	16	1,135.0
2010	1	17	1,140.0

You might be able to see that the data follows a seasonal pattern: for example there always seems to be a dip in Quarter 3 and a peak in Quarter 2. It is more obvious if plotted as a time series of sales against the consecutively numbered quarters.

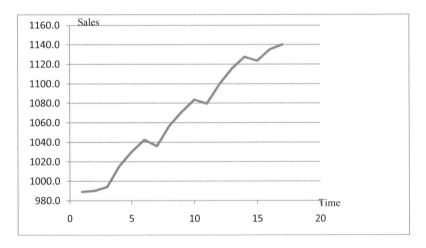

The moving average technique attempts to even out the seasonal variations. Here, because we seem to have data repeating every four readings a four-part moving average would be appropriate. If you were trading five days a week and wanted to even out the sales, a five-part moving average would be suitable.

The moving average is calculated as follows:

Take the first four figures and average them:

$$\frac{(989.0 + 990.0 + 994.0 + 1,015.0)}{4} = 997.0$$

Then move on one season:

$$\frac{(990.0 + 994.0 + 1,015.0 + 1,030.0)}{4} = 1,007.3$$

and so on, always averaging out all four seasons. Each average will include a high season and a low season.

That's rather tedious to do manually and Excel provides a function to do it automatically. To access this analysis function you must have the Excel Analysis ToolPak installed. If it is installed there will be an **Analysis>Data Analysis** tab in the **Data** section of the Ribbon.

If it is not already installed, you can install it as follows:

(1)   Click the **Microsoft Office Button** , and then click **Excel Options**.

(2)   Click **Add-Ins**, and then from the **Manage** box, select **Excel Add-Ins**.

(3)   Click **Go**.

(4)   In the **Add-Ins available** box, select the **Analysis ToolPak** check box, and then click *OK*.

Tip. If **Analysis ToolPak** is not listed in the **Add-Ins available** box, click **Browse** to locate it.

If you are prompted that the Analysis ToolPak is not currently installed on your computer, click **Yes** to install it. This may take a little time, so be patient!

---

(1)   Open the spreadsheet called Time series

(2)   Select **Data>Data analysis>Moving average**

(3)   Select D2:D18 as the **Input Range**

(4)   Enter 4 as the **Interval** (a four-part moving average)

(5)   Enter F2 as the **Output Range**

(6)   Check **Chart Output**

(7)   Click on **OK**

Don't worry about the error messages – the first three simply mean that you can't do a four-part average until you have four readings.

Move your cursor onto the moving average figures and move it down, one cell at a time to see how the averages move.

Notice on the graph how the Forecast line (the moving average) is much smoother than the actual figures. This makes predicting future sales much easier.

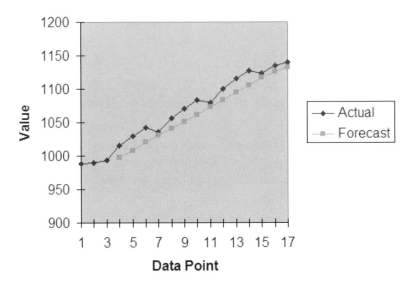

Moving Average

Mean, mode and median

These are three measures of what is known as the 'location' of data – they give an indication of whereabouts the data is clustered.

Mean (or arithmetic mean) is the ordinary average (add up the readings and divide by the number of readings).

Mode is the most frequently occurring item. For example, in a shoe shop, the arithmetic mean of shoe sizes is not much use. The shopkeeper is more interested in the most common shoe size.

Median is the value of the middle item if they are arranged in ascending or descending sequence. As well as medians you can have 'quartiles' (upper and lower) dividing the population into top one-quarter, lowest three-quarters (or *vice versa*) and 'deciles' (10:90 splits).

Excel allows all of these measures to be calculated (or identified) easily.

> (1) Open the spreadsheet called Student results.
>
> This lists the exam results of 23 students. They are currently displayed in alphabetical order. Don't worry about the column headed 'Bins' for now.
>
> Enter 'Mean' in cell A28, then make cell B28 active.

(2) Choose **Formulas>Σ AutoSum>Average** and accept the range offered. 58.56 is the arithmetic mean of the marks

(3) Enter 'Median' in cell A29, then make cell B29 active

(4) Choose **Formulas>More Functions>Statistical>MEDIAN**

(5) Enter the range B4:B26 for Number 1

You should see 57 as the median.

Check this by sorting the data into descending order by score, then counting up to the 12th student, Kate. (She's the middle student and scored 57).

(6) Enter 'Percentile' in cell A30, 0.75 in cell C30 and then make cell B30 active

(7) Choose **Formulas>More Functions>Statistical>PERCENTILE**

(8) Enter the range B4:B26 and C30 as the K value

The reported value is 68, the figure which divides the top quarter from the bottom three-quarters of students.

(9) Enter 'Mode' in cell A31 then make cell B31 active

(10) Choose **Formulas>More Functions>Statistical>Mode**

(11) Enter the range B4:B26

The reported value is 65 (that occurs more frequently than any other score).

Histograms

A histogram is a graph which shows the frequency with which certain values occur. Usually the values are grouped so that one could produce a histogram showing how many people were 160–165cm tall, how many >165–170, >170–175 and so on.

Excel can produce histogram analyses provided the Analysis ToolPak is installed. Installation was described earlier in the section about time series.

To demonstrate the histogram we will use the Student results spreadsheet again.

(1) Open the Student results spreadsheet if it is not already open.

You will see that in E5 to E13 is a column called 'Bins'. This describes the groupings that we want our results to be included in, so here we are going up the result in groups (bins) of ten percentage points at a time and the histogram will show how many results are in 0–10, 10–20, 20–30 etc.

(2) Choose **Data>Data Analysis>Histogram**

(3) Enter the range B4:B26 as the **Input Range**

(4)   Enter E5:E13 as the **Bin Range**

(5)   Choose **New Worksheet Ply** and enter 'Histogram analysis' in the white text box

(6)   Tick **Chart Output**

(7)   Click on **OK**

The new worksheet will show the data grouped into the 'bins' by frequency and also shows a histogram.

The spreadsheet 'Student results finished' shows the finished spreadsheet complete with histogram in the Histogram analysis sheet.

COMBINATION CHARTS

Excel allows you to combine two different charts into one. For example you may wish to compare sales to profits. This is also known as showing two graphs on one axis.

To do this we create a chart from our data as before.

(1)   Open the Combination chart spreadsheet from the downloaded files. This provides data for the number of sales of precious metal in 2009 and 2010. The price at which the precious metal is sold per kilo goes up and down according to the market.

(2)   Select the data that will go into your chart (cells A1 to C9)

(3)   Click Insert and then choose your chart type. For this example let's choose a **2D clustered column** chart. The chart doesn't really help us to understand the relationship between the two different sets of data.

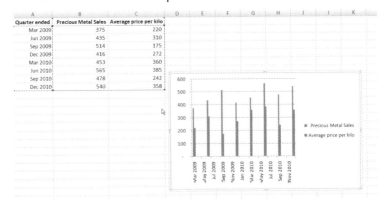

(4)   A more visual way of displaying the average price data might be to see it in a line set against the number of sales. So click on any Average price column, right click and select **Change Series Chart Type.**

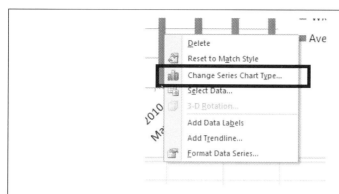

(5) Select **Line with Markers** and click **OK**. The chart will look like this:

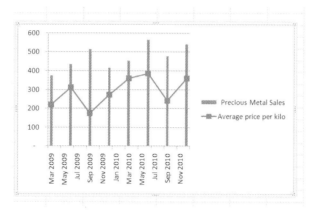

(6) The chart still does not make sense as the figures on the left axis are not comparing like with like. So we need to right click again an Average price marker and choose **Format Data Series**

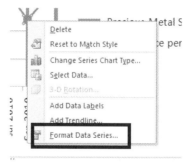

(7) Click **Secondary Axis**.

(8) Click **OK**.

(9) Take some time to play with the **Chart Tools**. Give the chart the name 'Precious Metal Sales' and label the axes. The vertical axis on the left should show the 'Number of sales', while the right hand axis should show the 'Price per kilo'.

You should end up with a chart that looks something like:

It can clearly be seen that the price per kilo dips in the third quarter of each year, something we could not easily determine without using the combination chart.

ERROR DETECTION AND CORRECTION

It is important to try to detect and correct errors before a spreadsheet is used to make decisions. We've already looked at some ways of trying to prevent wrong input (for example, data validation).

The final part of this chapter covers Excel's built-in help facility, error messages and ways to check that a spreadsheet has been constructed and is being used correctly.

Help

You can use Excel's Help window to quickly find the answer to any questions you may have while using Excel. You can access Help by clicking the **Help** button (the white question mark in the blue circle) in the top right corner of your spreadsheet or by pressing **F1**.

You can either type a search term directly into the white bar, or click on the **book icon** to access a table of help contents.

Table of contents

Or type query here

Take some time to explore the results when you type in different search terms. For example, if you found the section on What If analysis challenging, you could type 'What if' into the search bar to receive help on this topic.

Removing circular references

Circular references nearly always mean that there's a mistake in the logic of the spreadsheet. Here's an example:

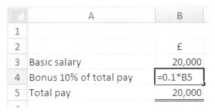

A warning will be displayed by Excel:

In our example, it is relatively easy to find the cause of the problem, but in a large spreadsheet it can be difficult. Clicking **OK** will provide help and will bring up a help screen referring you to **Formulas>Formula Auditing>Circular References** on the Ribbon.

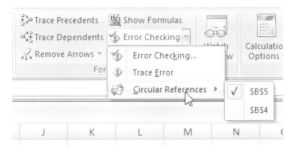

Using trace precedents

We saw earlier how to trace cells that provide data to a formula (precedents).

To recap, open the Precedent example 2 spreadsheet and click on cell D8. Then from the Ribbon select **Formulas>Formula Auditing>Trace Precedents**. A tracer arrow then appears linking the active cell with precedent cells.

	A	B	C	D
1				
2	£			
3	Region	Revenue	Costs	Gross profit
4	North	10,000	4,000	6,000
5	South	20,000	12,000	8,000
6	East	25,000	13,000	12,000
7	West	15,000	7,000	8,000
8		70,000	36,000	34,000

To identify the next level of precedents, remain in the active cell and from the Ribbon select **Formulas>Formula Auditing>Trace Precedents** again.

	A	B	C	D
1				
2	£			
3	Region	Revenue	Costs	Gross profit
4	North	10,000	4,000	6,000
5	South	20,000	12,000	8,000
6	East	25,000	13,000	12,000
7	West	15,000	7,000	8,000
8		70,000	36,000	34,000

Remember, once you are finished with tracing precedents and dependents you can remove the arrows by pressing the **Remove Arrows** button, or on the drop down arrow next to the **Remove Arrows** button to remove each arrow separately.

Rounding errors

The ability to display numbers in a variety of formats (eg to no decimal places) can result in a situation whereby totals that are correct may actually look incorrect.

Example: rounding errors

The following example shows how apparent rounding errors can arise.

	A	B	C
1	Petty cash		
2	Week ending 31/12/20X6		
3			£
4	Opening balance		231.34
5	Receipts		32.99
6	Payments		-104.67
7	Closing balance		159.66

	A	B	C
1	Petty cash		
2	Week ending 31/12/20X6		
3			£
4	Opening balance		231
5	Receipts		33
6	Payments		-105
7	Closing balance		160

Cell C7 contains the formula =SUM(C4:C6). The spreadsheet on the left shows the correct total to two decimal places. The spreadsheet on the right seems to be saying that 231 + 33 – 105 is equal to 160, which is not true, it's 159 (check it). The **reason for the discrepancy** is that both spreadsheets actually contain the values shown in the spreadsheet on the **left**.

However, the spreadsheet on the right has been formatted to display numbers with **no decimal places**. So, individual numbers display as the nearest whole number, although the actual value held by the spreadsheet and used in calculations includes the decimals.

The Round Function

One solution, that will prevent the appearance of apparent errors, is to use the **ROUND function**. The ROUND function has the following structure: ROUND (value, places). 'Value' is the value to be rounded. 'Places' is the number of places to which the value is to be rounded.

The difference between using the ROUND function and formatting a value to a number of decimal places is that using the ROUND function actually **changes** the **value**, while formatting only changes the **appearance** of the value.

In the example above, the ROUND function could be used as follows. The following formulae could be inserted in cells D4 to D7.

D4 = ROUND(C4,0)
D5 = ROUND(C5,0)
D6 = ROUND(C6,0)
D7 = Round (SUM(D4:D6),0)

Column C could then be hidden by highlighting the whole column (clicking on the C at the top of the column), then right clicking anywhere on the column and selecting **Hide**. Try this for yourself, hands-on.

D4			f_x	=ROUND(C4,0)

Book10

	A	B	D	E
1	Petty cash			
2	Week ending 31/12/20X6			
3				
4	Opening balance		231	
5	Receipts		33	
6	Payments		-105	
7	Closing balance		159	
8				

Note that using the ROUND function to eliminate decimals results in slightly inaccurate calculation totals (in our example 160 is actually 'more correct' than the 159 obtained using ROUND). For this reason, some people prefer not to use the function, and to make users of the spreadsheet aware that small apparent differences are due to rounding.

Identifying error values

Error checking can be turned on by **Office button>Excel options>Formulas** and checking **Enable background error checking**. There is a list that allows you to decide which errors to be highlighted. If a green triangle appears in a cell, then the cell contains an error.

#NUM!

Other information about the nature of the error will also be supplied:

#########	The column is not wide enough to hold the number. Widen the column or choose another format in which to display the number (no green triangle here as it is not a 'real' error – just a presentation problem).
#DIV/0!	Commonly caused by a formula attempting to divide a number by zero (perhaps because the divisor cell is blank).
#VALUE!	Occurs when a mathematical formula refers to a cell containing text, eg if cell A2 contains text the formula =A1+A2+A3 will return #VALUE!. Functions that operate on ranges (eg SUM) will not result in a #VALUE! error as they ignore text values.
#NAME?	The formula contains text that is not a valid cell address, range name or function name. Check the spelling of any functions used (eg by looking through functions under **Formulas>Insert Function**).

#REF!	The formula includes an invalid cell reference, for example a reference to cells that have subsequently been deleted.
	If you notice the reference immediately after a deletion, use **Ctrl+Z** to reverse the deletion.
#NUM!	This error is caused by invalid numeric values being supplied to a worksheet formula or function. For example, using a negative number with the SQRT (square root) function.
	To investigate, check the formula and function logic and syntax. The **Formula Auditing** toolbar may help this process (see below).
#N/A	A value is not available to a function or formula, for example omitting a required argument from a spreadsheet function. Again, the **Formula Auditing** toolbar may help the investigation process (see below).

Tracing and correcting errors

If you do see one of the above errors you can trace where it came from by clicking on the cell with the error, then, from the **Formulas** tab of the Ribbon, choose **Formula Auditing** and click the down arrow next to **Error Checking**. Lines will appear pointing to the data that has produced the error.

If you simply click the **Error Checking** button, it will automatically check the current worksheet and alert you to any errors.

Finally, you can click **Evaluate Formula** to be taken step by step through it so that you can identify the error.

CHAPTER OVERVIEW

- It is important to save and **backup your work regularly**. You can use **Save as** to give various versions of the same document different names.

- It is important to **control the security** of spreadsheets through passwords, locking (protecting) cells against unauthorised or accidental changes, data validation on input.

- Spreadsheet packages permit the user to work with **multiple sheets** that refer to each other. This is sometimes referred to as a three dimensional spreadsheet.

- Excel offers sophisticated data handling including **sorting, filtering, pivot tables** and **look-up tables**.

- **Combination charts** allow you to show two sets of data on one axis of your chart.

- Three tools, **Data tables, Scenarios** and **Goal seek,** are available to allow you to explore various results using different sets of values in one or more formulas.

- **Error detection** and prevention is important in spreadsheet design and testing. There are useful facilities available such as tracing precedents and dependents, identification of circular references, and error reports, as well as Excel's built-in help function.

TEST YOUR LEARNING

Test 1

What command is used to save a file under a different name?

Test 2

What part of the Ribbon do you go to set up checking procedures on the input of data?

Test 3

List three possible uses for a multi-sheet (3D) spreadsheet.

Test 4

What does filtering do?

Test 5

What is a trend line?

Test 6

What is the median?

chapter 3:
INTRODUCTION TO SPREADSHEETS (EXCEL 2003)

chapter coverage 📖

This chapter and the next introduce spreadsheets, using Excel 2003. Chapters 1 and 2 cover the same material using Excel 2007. You should study and work through *either* **chapters 1 and 2** *or* **chapters 3 and 4**, depending on the Excel software you have.

Spreadsheets have become indispensible tools for the presentation and analysis of accounting data. This chapter covers:

✍ An overview of spreadsheets.

✍ Essential basic skills that will allow you to move around a spreadsheet, enter and edit data, fill cells, and insert and delete columns and rows.

✍ An introduction to some of the many formulas and functions available within Excel 2003.

✍ Charts and graphs using the Chart Wizard.

✍ Spreadsheet presentation and documentation including adding titles, clear labelling of rows and columns and appropriate formatting to help make the spreadsheet, and any charts in the spreadsheet, easy to read and interpret.

INTRODUCTION

The vast majority of people who work in an accounting environment are required to use spreadsheets to perform their duties. This fact is reflected in the AAT Standards, which require candidates to be able to produce clear, well-presented spreadsheets, that utilise appropriate spreadsheet functions and formulae.

WHAT IS A SPREADSHEET?

Before we start to use a spreadsheet, it is important to gain an overview of what a spreadsheet can do. Soon, you will be asked to open a spreadsheet and to work through some hands-on exercises.

A spreadsheet is essentially an electronic piece of paper divided into **rows** (horizontal) and **columns** (vertical). The rows are numbered 1, 2, 3 . . . etc and the columns lettered A, B C . . . etc. Each individual area representing the intersection of a row and a column is called a '**cell**'. A cell's address consists of its row and column reference. For example, in the spreadsheet below the word '*Jan*' is in cell B2. The cell that the cursor is currently in or over is known as the 'active cell'. Active cells can be selected by clicking on them or using the arrow keys to move from one to the next.

The main examples of spreadsheet packages are Lotus 1-2-3 and Microsoft Excel. We will be referring to **Microsoft Excel**. The examples in this part of this book use **Excel 2003**. The first part of this book repeats the material but with reference to and using screen shots from **Excel 2007**.

A simple spreadsheet is shown below.

	A	B	C	D	E
1	BUDGETED SALES FIGURES				
2		Jan	Feb	Mar	Total
3		£'000	£'000	£'000	£'000
4	North	2,431	3,001	2,189	7,621
5	South	6,532	5,826	6,124	18,482
6	West	895	432	596	1,923
7	Total	9,858	9,259	8,909	28,026

Why use spreadsheets?

Spreadsheets provide a tool for calculating, analysing and manipulating numerical data. Spreadsheets make the calculation and manipulation of data easier and quicker. For example, the spreadsheet above has been set up to calculate the totals **automatically**. If you changed your estimate of sales in February for the North region to £3,296, when you input this figure in cell C4 the totals (in E4, C7 and E7) would change automatically.

Uses of spreadsheets

Spreadsheets can be used for a wide range of tasks. Some common applications of spreadsheets are:

- Management accounts
- Cash flow analysis and forecasting
- Reconciliations
- Revenue analysis and comparison
- Cost analysis and comparison
- Budgets and forecasts

Spreadsheet software also provides very basic database capabilities which allow simple records to be recorded, sorted and searched.

BASIC SKILLS

In this section we explain some **basic spreadsheet skills**.

You should read this section while sitting at a computer and trying out the skills we describe '**hands-on**'.

The menus

Start Microsoft Excel by double-clicking on the **Microsoft Office Excel 2003 (Excel) icon** or button on the computer desktop:

or by choosing Excel from the **Start** menu (possibly from within the **Microsoft Office** group).

The menu bar

When you first open Excel, you will see a screen with a menu bar that looks something like:

Some customisation is possible, so yours might not look quite as shown above. For example, instead of having two lines of buttons you might have just one. Some of the buttons shown above might not be shown on your version either. Don't worry – buttons can be added, removed or moved onto another line by using the small drop-down button at the end of the menu bar:

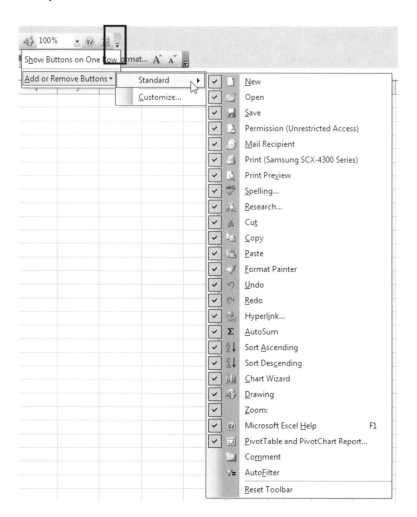

Workbooks and worksheets

At the bottom left of the spreadsheet window you will see tabs which are known as **Worksheets**:

When **New** is selected from the **File** menu, a new **workbook** is created.

The **workbook** consists of one or more **worksheets**. Think of worksheets as **pages** which make up the workbook. By default a new Excel workbook starts out with three worksheets, although this can be changed (see later).

This can provide a very convenient way of organising information. For example, consider a business consisting of three branches. Worksheets 2–4 could hold budget information separately for each branch. When entering formulae into cells it is possible to refer to cells in other worksheets within the workbook so it would then be possible for Worksheet 1 to show the totals of the budget information for the whole business. Effectively, a three dimensional structure can be set up. We look at this in more detail later.

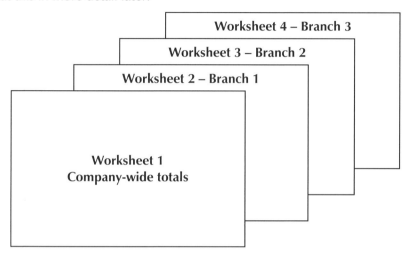

Opening an existing workbook

You can open an existing workbook file by using the menu commands **File>Open** and then navigating to the location of the file and double clicking on it.

If you open more than one workbook, each will open in a new window. To swap between open workbooks, click on **Window** on the menu bar and choose the workbook you want from the list of file names are the bottom of the menu.

Closing a workbook

There are two ways to close a spreadsheet file:

(1) Click on **File>Close**

(2) Click on either the **'x'** in the top right hand corner of the window or the one just below it.

 OR

In both cases, if you have made any changes to the spreadsheet you will be asked if you want to save them. Choose **Yes** to save any changes (this will overwrite the existing file), **No** to close the file without saving any changes, or **Cancel** to return to the spreadsheet.

Cell contents

The contents of any cell can be one of the following:

(a) **Text**. A text cell usually contains **words**. Numbers that do not represent numeric values for calculation purposes (eg a Part Number) may be entered in a way that tells Excel to treat the cell contents as text. To do this, enter an apostrophe before the number eg '451.

(b) **Values**. A value is a **number** that can be used in a calculation.

(c) **Formulae**. A formula **refers to other cells** in the spreadsheet, and performs some type of computation with them. For example, if cell C1 contains the formula =A1 – B1, cell C1 will display the result of the calculation subtracting the contents of cell B1 from the contents of cell A1. In Excel, a formula always begins with an equals sign: = . This alerts the program that what follows is a formula and not text or a value. There is a wide range of formulae and functions available.

Formulas and the formula bar

Open the workbook called ExcelExample1. This is one of the files available for download from www.bpp.com/aatspreadsheets. You can open a file by using the menu commands:

File>Open

then navigating to and double clicking on the file called ExcelExample1.

Note. Throughout this text we will want the spreadsheet to recalculate every time a figure is changed. If it does not do this then:

(1) On the *Tools* menu, click *Options*, and then click the *Calculation* tab.

(2) Under *Calculation*, select *Automatic*.

E4		f_x =B4+C4+D4		
	A	B	C	D	E
1	BUDGETED SALES FIGURES				
2		Jan	Feb	Mar	Total
3		£'000	£'000	£'000	£'000
4	North	2,431	3,001	2,189	7,621
5	South	6,532	5,826	6,124	18,482
6	West	895	432	596	1,923
7	Total	9,858	9,259	8,909	28,026

Formula shown in formula bar

You should see the worksheet illustrated above. Click on cell E4.

Look at the formula bar.

Note. If the formula bar is not visible, choose **View** from the top line of the menu and check **Formula Bar**.

Note the important difference between:

(1)   What is shown in cell E4: 7,621

(2)   What is actually in cell E4: this is shown in the formula bar and it tells us that cell E4 is the result of adding together the contents of cells B4, C4 and D4

The formula bar allows you to see and edit the contents of the active cell. The bar also shows, on the left hand side, the cell address of the active cell (E4 in the example above).

> Select different cells to be the active cell by using the up/down/right/left arrows on your keyboard or by clicking directly on the cell you want to be active. Look at what is in the cell and what is shown in the formula bar.
>
> The F5 key is useful for moving around within large spreadsheets. If you press the function key **F5**, a **Go To** dialogue box will allow you to specify the cell address you would like to move to. Try this out.
>
> Also experiment by holding down Ctrl and pressing each of the direction arrow keys in turn to see where you end up. Try using the **Page Up** and **Page Down** keys and also try **Home** and **End** and Ctrl + these keys. Try **Tab** and **Shift + Tab**, too. These are all useful shortcuts for moving quickly from one place to another in a large spreadsheet.

Examples of spreadsheet formulae

Formulae in Microsoft Excel follow a specific syntax. All Excel formulae start with the equals sign =, followed by the elements to be calculated (the operands) and the calculation operators (such as +, -, /, *). Each operand can be a:

- Value that does not change (a constant value, such as the VAT rate)

- Cell or range reference to a range of cells

- Name (a named cell, such as 'VAT')

- Worksheet function (such as 'AVERAGE', which will work out the average value of defined values)

Formulae can be used to perform a variety of calculations. Here are some examples:

(a)   =C4*5. This formula **multiplies** the value in C4 by 5. The result will appear in the cell holding the formula.

(b)   =C4*B10. This **multiplies** the value in C4 by the value in B10.

(c)   =C4/E5. This **divides** the value in C4 by the value in E5. * means multiply and / means divide by.

(d)   =C4*B10–D1. This **multiplies** the value in C4 by that in B10 and then subtracts the value in D1 from the result. Note that generally Excel will perform multiplication and division before addition or subtraction. If in any doubt, use brackets (parentheses): =(C4*B10) – D1.

(e) =C4*117.5%. This **adds** 17.5% to the value in C4. It could be used to calculate a price including 17.5% VAT.

(f) =(C4+C5+C6)/3. Note that the **brackets** mean Excel would perform the addition first. Without the brackets, Excel would first divide the value in C6 by 3 and then add the result to the total of the values in C4 and C5.

(g) = 2^2 gives you 2 **to the power** of 2, in other words 22. Likewise = 2^3 gives you 2 cubed and so on.

(h) = 4^ (1/2) gives you the **square root** of 4. Likewise 27^(1/3) gives you the cube root of 27 and so on.

Displaying spreadsheet formulae

It is sometimes useful to see all formulae held in your spreadsheet to enable you to see how the spreadsheet works. There are two ways of making Excel **display the formulae** held in a spreadsheet.

(a) You can 'toggle' between the two types of display by pressing **Ctrl +`** (the latter is the key above the Tab key). Press Ctrl +` again to go back to the previous display.

(b) You can also click on **Tools>Formula Auditing>Formula Auditing Mode**. The formulas for the spreadsheet we viewed earlier are shown below.

	A	B	C	D	E
1	BUDGETED SALES FIG				
2		Jan	Feb	Mar	Total
3		£'000	£'000	£'000	£'000
4	North	2431	3001	2189	=B4+C4+D4
5	South	6532	5826	6124	=B5+C5+D5
6	West	895	432	596	=B6+C6+D6
7	Total	=B4+B5+B6	=C4+C5+C6	=D4+D5+D6	=E4+E5+E6
8					

The importance of formulae

Look carefully at the example above and note which cells have formulae in them. It is important to realise that:

- If a cell contains a value, such as sales for North in January, then that data is entered as a number.

- If a cell shows the result of a calculation based on values in other cells, such as the total sales for January, then that cell contains a formula.

This is vital, because now if North's January sales were changed to, say, 2,500, the total would be automatically updated to show 9,927. Also the total for North would change to 7,690.

> Try that out by clicking on cell B4 to make it active, then typing 2,500, followed by the Enter key. You should see both the totals change.
>
> Now re-enter the original figure of 2,432 into cell B4.

Similarly, if a number is used more than once, for example a tax rate, it will be much better if the number is input to one cell only. Any other calculations making use of that value should refer to that cell. That way, if the tax rate changes, you only have to change it in one place in the spreadsheet (where it was originally entered) and any calculations making use of it will automatically change.

Your first function

In the example above, totals were calculated using a formula such as:

=+B4+C4+D4

That is fine provided there are not too many items to be included in the total. Imagine, the difficulty if you had to find the total of 52 weeks for a year. Adding up rows or columns is made much easier by using the SUM function. Instead of the formula above, we could place the following calculation in cell E4:

=SUM(B4:D4)

This produces the sum of all the cells in the range B4 to D4. Now it is much easier to add up a very long row of figures (for example, SUM(F5:T5)) or a very long column of figures (for example, SUM(B10:B60)).

There are three ways in which the SUM function can be entered. One way is simply to type =SUM(B4:D4) when E4 is the active cell. However, there is a more visual and perhaps more accurate way.

> (1) Make E4 the active cell by moving the cursor to it using the arrow keys or by clicking on it.
>
> (2) Type =Sum(
>
> (3) Click on cell B4
>
> (4) Type a colon :
>
> (5) Click on cell D4
>
> (6) Close the bracket by typing)
>
> (7) Press the Enter key

Another way is to use the AutoSum button, which we cover later.

Editing cell contents

Cell D5 of ExcelExample1 currently contains the value 6,124. If you wish to change the value in that cell from 6,124 to 6,154 there are four options (you have already used the first method).

(1) Activate cell D5, **type** 6,154 and press **Enter**.

(2) To undo this and try the next option press **Ctrl + Z**: this will always undo what you have just done (a very useful shortcut)

(3) **Double-click** in cell D5. The cell will keep its thick outline but you will now be able to see a vertical line flashing in the cell. You can move this line by using the direction arrow keys or the Home and the End keys. Move it to just after the 2, press the **backspace** key on the keyboard and then type 5. Then press **Enter**. (Alternatively, move the vertical line to just in front of the 2, press the **Delete** key on the keyboard, then type 5, followed by the **Enter** key.)

(4) When you have tried this press **Ctrl + Z** to undo it.

(5) **Click once** before the number 6,124 in the formula bar. Again, you will get the vertical line which can be moved back and forth to allow editing as in (3) above.

(6) Activate cell D4 and press **F2** at the top of your keyboard. The vertical line cursor will be flashing in cell D4 at the end of the figures entered there and this can be used to edit the cell contents, as above.

Deleting cell contents

There are a number of ways to delete the contents of a cell:

(a) Make the cell the active cell and press the **Delete** button. The contents of the cell will disappear.

(b) Go to **Edit>Clear** and you will see various options appear. Click **Contents**. You can also achieve this by **right clicking** the cell and choosing **Clear contents**.

Any cell formatting (for example, cell colour or border) will not be removed when using either of these methods. To remove formatting click **Edit>Clear>Formats**. If you want to remove the formatting *and* the contents, click **All**.

Ranges of cells

A range of cells can occupy a single column or row or can be a rectangle of cells. The extent of a range is defined by the rectangle's top left cell reference and the bottom right cell reference. If the range is within a single row or column, it is defined by the references of the start and end cells.

Defining a range is very useful as you can then manipulate many cells at once rather than having to go to each one individually.

The following shows that a rectangular range of cells has been selected from C4 to D6. The range consists of three rows and two columns.

	A	B	C	D	E
1	BUDGETED SALES FIGURES				
2		Jan	Feb	Mar	Total
3		£'000	£'000	£'000	£'000
4	North	2,431	3,001	2,189	7,621
5	South	6,532	5,826	6,124	18,482
6	West	895	432	596	1,923
7	Total	9,858	9,259	8,909	28,026

There are several ways of selecting ranges. Try the following.

(1) Click on cell C4, but hold the mouse button down. Drag the cursor down and to the right until the required range has been selected. Then release the mouse button. Now press the **Delete** key. All the cells in this range are cleared of their contents.

(2) Reverse this by **Ctrl+Z** and deselect the range by clicking on any single cell.

(3) Click on cell C4 (release the mouse button). Hold down the **Shift** key and press the **down** and **right hand arrows** until the correct range is highlighted.

Deselect the range by clicking on any single cell.

(4) Click on cell C4 (release the mouse button). Hold down the **Shift** key and click on cell D6.

Deselect the range by clicking on any single cell.

Sometimes you may want to select an entire row or column:

(5) Say you wanted to select row 3, perhaps to change all the occurrences of £'000 to a bold font. Position your cursor over the figure 3 defining row 3 and click. All of row 3 is selected. Clicking on the **B** on the formatting toolbar will make the entire row bold:

Whole spreadsheet selection

A3		f_x				
	A	B	C	D	E	F
1	BUDGETED SALES FIGURES					
2		Jan	Feb	Mar	Total	
3		£'000	£'000	£'000	£'000	
4	North	2,431	3,001	2,189	7,621	
5	South	6,532	5,826	6,124	18,482	
6	West	895	432	596	1,923	
7	Total	9,858	9,259	8,909	28,026	
8						

> Sometimes you may want to select every cell in the worksheet, perhaps to put everything into a different font:
>
> (6) Click on the blank box at top left of the cells (indicated above). Alternatively you can select the active cells using **Ctrl + A**.

Filling a range of cells

There are a number of labour-saving shortcuts which allow you to quickly fill ranges of cells with headings (such as £'000, or month names) and with patterns of numbers. You can keep the ExcelExercise1 spreadsheet open throughout the following activities and simply open a new spreadsheet on which to experiment.

(1) Create a new spreadsheet by clicking the button shown below:

(2) Make cell B3 active and type Jan (or January) into it.

(3) Position the cursor at the bottom right of cell B3 (you will see a black + when you are at the right spot– this is often referred to as the **fill handle**).

(4) Hold down the mouse button and drag the cursor rightwards, until it is under row G. Release the mouse button.

The month names will automatically fill across.

(5) Using the same technique, fill B4 to G4 with £.

(6) Type 'Region' into cell 3A.

(7) Type the figure 1 into cell A5 and 2 into cell A6. Select the range A5–A6 and obtain the black cross at the bottom right of cell A6. Hold down the mouse key and drag the cursor down to row 10. Release the mouse button.

The figures 1–6 will automatically fill down column A.

Note: If 1 and 3 had been entered into A5 and C6, then 1, 3, 5, 7, 9, 11 would automatically appear. This does **not** work if just the figure 1 is entered into A5.

The AutoSum button Σ

We will explain how to use the AutoSum button by way of a simple example.

(1) Clear your worksheet (**Select all>Delete**).

(2) Enter the following figures in cells A1:B5. (**Hint.** Instead of pressing return after each figure, you can press the down or right arrow to enter the figure and to move to the next cell).

	A	B
1	400	582
2	250	478
3	359	264
4	476	16
5	97	125

(3) Make cell B6 the active cell and select the **Σ** button. Click the small drop-down arrow and select Σ **Sum**.

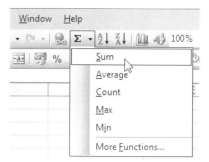

(4) The formula =SUM(B1:B5) will appear in the cell. Above cell B6 you will see a flashing dotted line around cells B1:B5. Accept the suggested formula by hitting Enter. 1,465 should appear in B6. Alternatively, you can simply click on the **Σ** (**AutoSum**) symbol itself (see later)

(5) Next, make cell A6 the active cell and repeat the operation for that column. The number 1582 should appear in cell A6.

(6) Now delete the two totals.

Copying and pasting formulae

You have already seen that formulae are extremely important in spreadsheet construction. In Excel it is very easy to define a formula once and then apply it to a wide range of cells. As it is applied to different cells the cell references in the formula are automatically updated. Say, that in the above example, you wanted to multiply together each row of figures in columns A and B and to display the answer in the equivalent rows of column C.

(1) Make C1 the active cell.

(2) Type =, then click on cell A1, then type * and click on cell B1.

(3) Press Enter

The formula =A1*B1 should be shown in the formula bar, and the amount 232,800 should be shown in C1.

(4) Make C1 the active cell and obtain the black + by positioning the cursor at the bottom right of that cell.

(5) Hold down the mouse button and drag the cursor down to row 5.

(6) Release the mouse button.

Look at the formulae in column C. You will see that the cell references change as you move down the column, updating as you move from row to row.

	File	Edit	View	Insert	Format	Too

Arial 10 **B** *I*

C3 ▼ *fx* =A3*B3

	A	B	C	D
1	400	582	232800	
2	250	478	119500	
3	359	264	94776	
4	476	£16	7616	
5	97	125	12125	

It is also possible to copy whole blocks of cells, with formulae being updated in a logical way.

(1) Make A1 the active cell and select the range A1:C5, for example, by dragging the cursor down and rightwards.

(2) Press **Ctrl+C** (the standard Windows Copy command) or click on the **Copy** symbol in the toolbar.

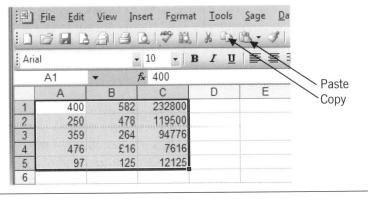

	File	Edit	View	Insert	Format	Tools	Sage	Da

Arial 10 **B** *I* **U**

A1 ▼ *fx* 400

Paste
Copy

	A	B	C	D	E
1	400	582	232800		
2	250	478	119500		
3	359	264	94776		
4	476	£16	7616		
5	97	125	12125		
6					

(3) Make E7 the active cell and press **Ctrl+V** or click on the paste button. E7 will become the top right cell of the copied rectangle and will hold 400.

(4) Now, look at the formulae shown in cell G7. It will show =E7*F7. So all cell references in the formulae have been updated relative to one another. This type of copying is called **relative copying**.

(5) **Delete** the range E7:G7.

Paste special

Sometimes you don't want to copy formulae and you only want to copy the displayed values. This can be done using **Paste special**.

Open the spreadsheet called Paste special example from the files available for download at www.bpp.com/aatspreadsheets.

You will see a simple inventory-type application listing quantities, prices and values. The values are obtained by formulae multiplying together prices and quantities.

Say that you just want to copy the values of cells D3:D8, without the underlying formulae.

(1) Select the range D3:D8

(2) Press **Ctrl+C** or the **Copy** icon on the toolbar

(3) Right-click on cell C12 to make it active, and choose **Paste Special** from the list.

(4) Check the **Values** radio button

(5) Click **OK**

The list of figures will be pasted, but if you look in the formula bar, you will see that they are just figures: there are no formulae there.

Note: If you change a quantity or price in the original table, the figures you have just pasted will not change: they have become pure numbers and do not link back to their source.

Inserting and deleting columns and rows

Often you will need to insert or delete whole rows or columns in spreadsheets. This can easily be done and, sometimes formulae are correctly updated – but they should always be checked. For this exercise we will go back to using the ExcelExample1 spreadsheet.

Close the spreadsheet you have recently been working on and go back to (using the tabs across bottom of the screen) or reopen the spreadsheet ExcelExample1.

Let us assume that we have a new region, East and that we want this to be in a row lying between North and South.

(1) Select row 5, by clicking on the 5, then click the right mouse button ('right click') and select **Insert**. You will see rows 5, 6 and 7 move down.

(2) Make B8 the active cell and you will see that the formula in the formula bar is =B4+B6+B7. If we were to put the figures for East into row 5 then those would **not** be correctly included in the total, though B5 has been updated to B6 etc.

(3) Reverse the last step (**Ctrl+Z**).

(4) Now, in cell B7 insert =SUM(B4:B6).

(5) Copy B4 across columns C7 to E7 (black cross and drag across).

(6) Check the formulas that are in cells C7 to E7 to ensure they have all been updated.

(7) Insert a whole row above row 5 (**Select row 5>right click>Insert**).

(8) Inspect the formulae in row 8, the new total row.

The formulae in the total row will now be showing =SUM(B4:B7), =SUM(C4:C7), etc. In this case the new row will be included in the total. Effectively, the range over which the totals are calculated has been 'stretched'. Depending how your copy of Excel is set up, you may notice little green triangles in row 8. If so, place your cursor on one and press the exclamation symbol. The triangles are warning that you have included empty cells in your total – not a problem here, but it might have been in some cases. Don't worry if the triangles aren't showing.

(9) Finally delete row 5. Select the whole row by clicking on the 5, then right click and choose **Delete** from the menu.

The cells below Row 5 will move up and the SUM formulae are again updated.

New columns can also be added. Say that we now wanted to include April in the results.

(1) Replace the current formula in E4 with =SUM(B4:D4).

(2) Copy the formula in E4 down through columns 5, 6 and 7. Check that the correct formulae are in cells E4–E7.

(3) Select column E, by clicking on the E, then click the right mouse button ('right click') and select **Insert**. You will see column E move to the right.

(4)   Inspect the formulae now in Column F, the new total column.

You will see that the formula in F7 still says = SUM(B4:D4). It has **not been updated** for the extra column.

So, if an extra row or column is inserted in the middle of a range, the formulae is updated because the new row or column probably (but not always) becomes part of the range that has to be added up.

However, if the extra row or column is added at the end of a range (or the start) the formula will not be updated to include that. That's reasonably logical as new items at the very start or end have a greater chance of being headings or something not part of the range to be included in a calculation.

So:

**Whenever columns or rows are added or deleted,
check that formulae affected remain correct**.

Tracing precedents and dependents

As spreadsheets are developed it can become difficult to be sure where figures come from and go to (despite being able to display formulae in all the cells). A useful technique is to make use of the trace precedents and trace dependents options. These are available in **Tools>Formula Auditing**.

(1)   Open the Precedent example spreadsheet from the downloaded files and make cell F4 active.

(2)   Choose the **Tools>Formula Auditing>Trace Precedents** from the menu bar.

You should see:

	A	B	C	D	E	F
	F4		fx =SUM(B4:D4)			
1	BUDGETED SALES FIGURES					
2		Jan	Feb	Mar		Total
3		£'000	£'000	£'000		£'000
4	North	2,431	3,001	2,189		7,621
5	South	6,532	5,826	6,124		18,482
6	West	895	432	596		1,923
7	Total	9,858	9,259	8,909		28,026

Now it is very obvious that anything in column E, like April figures will not be included in the total.

(3)   Click on **Tools>Formula Auditing>Remove All Arrows**.

(4)   Make B4 the active cell.

(5) Click on **Tools>Formula Auditing>Trace Dependents**. This will show what cells make use of this cell:

	B4	▾		_fx_ 2431			
	A	B	C	D	E	F
1	BUDGETED SALES FIGURES					
2		Jan	Feb	Mar		Total
3		£'000	£'000	£'000		£'000
4	North	2,431	3,001	2,189		7,621
5	South	6,532	5,826	6,124		18,482
6	West	895	432	596		1,923
7	Total	9,858	9,259	8,909		28,026

Changing column width and height

You may occasionally find that a cell is not wide enough to display its contents. When this occurs, the cell displays a series of hashes ######. There are several ways to deal with this problem:

- Column widths can be adjusted by positioning the mouse pointer at the head of the column, directly over the little line dividing two columns. The mouse **pointer** will change to a **cross** with a double-headed arrow through it. Hold down the left mouse button and, by moving your mouse, stretch or shrink the column until it is the right width. Alternatively, you can double click when the double-headed arrow appears and the column will automatically adjust to the optimum width.

- Highlight the columns you want to adjust and choose **Format>Column> Width** from the menu and set the width manually

- Highlight the columns you want to adjust and choose **Format>Column> Autofit Selection** from the menu and set the width to fit the contents.

Setting column heights works similarly.

Dates

You can insert the current date into a cell by **Ctrl + ;** (semicolon).

You can insert the current time by **Ctrl+Shift + ;**.

You can insert date and time by first inserting the date, release Ctrl, press space, insert the time.

The date can be formatted by going to **Home>Number>Format Cells Date** and choosing the format required.

Once a date is entered it is easy to produce a sequence of dates.

In a new worksheet, insert the date 1/1/2011 in cell A1.

(1) Format so as to show 01 January 2011.

(2) In A2, insert the date 8/1/2011 and format it to appear as 08 January 2011

(3) Select cells A1 and A2.

(4) Position the cursor on the bottom right of cell A2 (a black + will appear).

(5) Hold down the mouse button and drag the mouse down to A12.

The cells should fill with dates seven days apart.

(If you see ###### in a cell it means that column A is too narrow, so widen it as explained above.)

Naming cells

It can be difficult to always have to refer to a cell co-ordinate, eg C12. Cell C12 might contain the VAT rate and it would be more natural (and less error prone) to refer to a name like 'VAT'.

(1) Open the worksheet called Name example.

(2) Make cell B3 the active one

(3) Click **Insert>Name>Define**

(4) Accept the offered name, 'VAT' that Excel has picked up from the neighbouring cell.

(5) Highlight the range D4:D7, and click on **Insert>Name>Define**

(6) In E4 enter =Net*(1 + VAT).

(7) Copy E4 into E5:E7.

You will see the formula bar refers to names. This makes understanding a spreadsheet much easier.

A list of names can be seen using the **Insert>Name>Define** and looking at the names under **Names in workbook** together with their references.

Keyboard shortcuts

Here are a few tips to quickly improve the **appearance** of your spreadsheets and speed up your work, using only the keyboard. These are all alternatives to clicking the relevant button on the formatting toolbar.

To do any of the following to a cell or range of cells, first **select** the cell or cells and then:

(a) Press **Ctrl + B** to make the cell contents **bold**.

(b) Press **Ctrl + I** to make the cell contents *italic*.

(c) Press **Ctrl + U** to <u>underline</u> the cell contents.

(d) Press **Ctrl + C** to **Copy** the contents of the cells.

(e) Move the cursor and press **Ctrl + V** to **paste** the cell you just copied into the new active cell or cells.

SPREADSHEET CONSTRUCTION

All spreadsheets need to be planned and then constructed carefully. More complex spreadsheet models should include some documentation that explains how the spreadsheet is set-up and how to use it.

There can be a feeling that, because the spreadsheet carries out calculations automatically, results will be reliable. However, there can easily be errors in formulae, errors of principle and errors in assumptions. All too often, spreadsheets offer a reliable and quick way to produce nonsense.

Furthermore, it is rare for only one person to have to use or adapt a spreadsheet and proper documentation is important if other people are to be able to make efficient use of it.

The following should be kept in separate identifiable areas of the spreadsheet:

(1) An inputs and assumptions section containing the variables (eg the amount of a loan and the interest rate, planned mark-ups, assumptions about growth rates).

(2) A calculations section containing formulae.

(3) The results section, showing the outcome of the calculations.

Sometimes it is convenient to combine (2) and (3).

It is also important to:

(1) Document data sources. For example, where did the assumed growth rate come from? If you don't know that, how will you ever test the validity of that data and any results arising from it.

(2) Explain calculation methods. This is particularly important if calculations are complex or have to be done in a specified way.

(3) Explain the variables used in functions. Some functions require several input variables (arguments) and may not be familiar to other users.

(4)   Set out the spreadsheet clearly, using underlinings, colour, bold text etc to assist users.

In simple spreadsheets the calculations and results can often be combined. Here is an example arranged in this way (in your downloaded files this example is called 'Mortgage'):

	D9	▾		f_x =PMT(C3/12,C5*12,C4)							
	A	B	C	D	E	F	G	H	I J		K
1	Assumptions										
2											
3	Annual interest rate		10%								
4	Amount of loan (£)		20,000								
5	Period of loan		20								
6											
7	Calculation of monthly repayments over a reducing balance mortgage lasting (years)							20			
8											
9	Monthly repayment			-£193.00	Uses the PMT function where:						
10					Monthly interest rate = annual rate/12						
11					There are 12 x Number of years mortgage payments						
12					The amount paid pays of the mortgage precisely						
13											

This example makes use of the **Cell Comment** facility (see below) in cell D9. The explanatory message appears when the cursor is over cell D9.

If we wanted to carry out the calculation for loan of a different amount, or at a different interest rate, or for a different period, we would simply have to **overwrite the figures in the assumptions/variables section** of the spreadsheet with the new figures to calculate the revised monthly repayments.

Of course, you may not want the assumptions to be at the top left of the spreadsheet and therefore the first thing seen. However, the location of the assumptions must be made very clear to users.

Work through the example that follows.

Example: constructing a cash flow projection

You want to set up a simple six-month cash flow projection in such a way that you can use it to estimate how the **projected cash balance** figures will **change** in total when any **individual item** in the projection is **altered**. You have the following information.

(a)   Sales were £45,000 per month in 20X5, falling to £42,000 in January 20X6. Thereafter they are expected to increase by 3% per month (ie February will be 3% higher than January, and so on).

(b)   Debts are collected as follows.

(i)   60% in month following sale.
(ii)   30% in second month after sale.

121

(iii) 7% in third month after sale.

(iv) 3% remains uncollected.

(c) Purchases are equal to cost of sales, set at 65% of sales.

(d) Overheads were £6,000 per month in 20X5, rising by 5% in 20X6.

(e) Opening cash is an overdraft of £7,500.

(f) Dividends: £10,000 final dividend on 20X5 profits payable in May.

(g) Capital purchases: plant costing £18,000 will be ordered in January. 20% is payable with order, 70% on delivery in February and the final 10% in May.

Setting up the assumptions area

These assumptions have been set up in an opening spreadsheet for you.

---

(1) Open the downloaded file called Cash Flow Exercise – Assumptions (**File>Open**).

(2) Move the cursor over the items in columns B and G. These columns contain the numbers or values making up the assumptions.

Each of these figures has to be kept in a separate cell so that it can be separately referenced in subsequent calculations. There's no point, for example, having "Historical monthly sales 2005 (£) 45,000" all in one cell because we will have to use the amount 45,000 later.

Note the opening cash balance is -7,500 to indicate an overdraft.

We have shaded the assumptions area to make it distinct from other parts of the spreadsheet. You can change the colour of a cell, or range of cells, by selecting the cells you want to change then going to either:

(a) **Format>Cells>Patterns** and choosing a colour, or

(b) Clicking on the down arrow next to the 'paint pot' icon on the formatting toolbar and choosing a colour from there.

Headings and layout

Next we will enter the various **headings** required for the cash flow projection.

Look at the picture below. Try to recreate this in the spreadsheet you have just opened starting with adding the heading 'The cash flow' in call A15. Make sure you use exactly the same rows and columns as these are referred to later. The notes following the graphic may give you some help.

You want your spreadsheet to look like this:

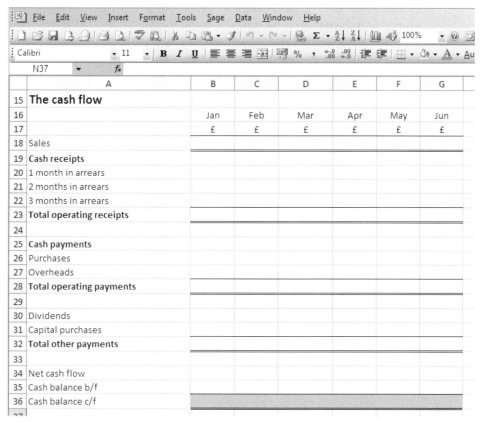

	A	B	C	D	E	F	G
15	**The cash flow**						
16		Jan	Feb	Mar	Apr	May	Jun
17		£	£	£	£	£	£
18	Sales						
19	**Cash receipts**						
20	1 month in arrears						
21	2 months in arrears						
22	3 months in arrears						
23	**Total operating receipts**						
24							
25	**Cash payments**						
26	Purchases						
27	Overheads						
28	**Total operating payments**						
29							
30	Dividends						
31	Capital purchases						
32	**Total other payments**						
33							
34	Net cash flow						
35	Cash balance b/f						
36	Cash balance c/f						

Note the following points.

(a) Column A is wider to allow longer items of text to be entered. Depending on how your copy of Excel is set up, this might happen automatically or you may have to drag the line between the A and B columns to the right.

(b) We have used a **simple style for headings**. Headings tell users what data relates to and what the spreadsheet 'does'. We have made some words **bold**, increased the size of some fonts and centralised others. This can be done by using the buttons in the **Font** group on the formatting toolbar (see below) or by selecting **Format>Cells>Font**.

(c) When **text** is entered into a cell it is usually **left aligned** (as for example in column A). We have **centred** the headings for months and the '£' signs above each column by highlighting the cells and using the relevant buttons in the **Font** group or accessing **Format> Cells>Alignment**.

Note that if you want a heading to span across two or more columns, select the cell with the text and the cells you want the heading to appear over and click **Format> Cells>Alignment** or click on the **Merge and Center** icon on the formatting toolbar.

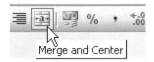

(d) **Numbers** should be **right aligned** in cells. This usually happens automatically when you enter a number into a cell.

(e) We have left **spaces** in certain rows (after blocks of related items) to make the spreadsheet **easier to use and read**.

(f) Totals have been highlighted by a single line above and a double line below. This can be done by highlighting the relevant cells then going to **Format>Cells>Border**.

First, select the style, then the border to apply it to. For example, to have a double line along the bottom side of a cell click the bottom right style, then click the lower border. An upper line can be added to the cell by selecting a single line then clicking the upper border.

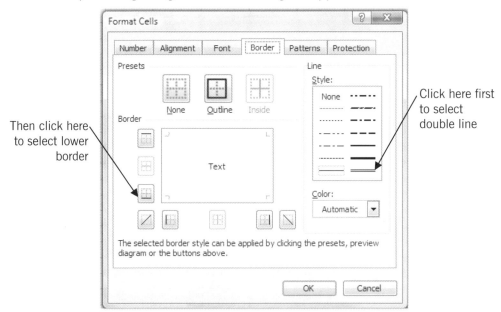

Alternatively, highlight the relevant cells, go to the **Borders** icon on the formatting toolbar and click on the drop-down arrow to access the available borders. If you click on the icon itself the default border is a border along the bottom of the cell.

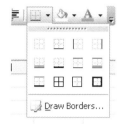

Inserting formulae

The next step is to enter the **formulae** required. For example, in cell B23 you want total operating receipts, =SUM(B20:B22). Similarly, the sales in February (cell C18) would be the sales in January increased by the assumed rate of growth of 3%.

You may be tempted to insert the formula =B18*1.03 in cell C18.

Similarly, in D18 you could put the formula = C18*1.03.

This would work, but would be poor practice. Think what would happen if you wanted to see the effect of a 5% growth rate: every formula in row 18 would have to be altered to include 1.05 rather than 1.03.

Remember what we said before: **always try to enter a variable that will be 'used' many times, such as a growth rate assumption, once only. Other cells should refer back to the cell containing that variable**.

Here, we already have the growth rate in cell B7 so the formula in cell C18 could be =B18*B7, and the formula in cell D18 could be =C18*B7. Now if we change the contents of B7 from 3% to 5% the spreadsheet is automatically updated for the new growth rate assumption.

The quick way to insert a series of formulae is to type in the initial one and then to copy across a row or down a column. You may remember that cell references are cleverly updated as you move along the row or column. (This was called relative copying.) However, that will get us into trouble here. If cell C18 contains the formula =B18*B7 and that is copied one cell to the right, into column D, the formula will become =C18*C7.

The C18 reference is correct because we are progressing along the row, one month at a time, but the C7 reference is incorrect. The location of the growth rate does not move: it is **absolute**. To prevent a cell reference being updated during the copying process put a '$' sign in front of the row and>or column reference.

A reference like $A1 will mean that column A is always referred to as you copy across the spreadsheet. If you were to copy down, the references would be updated to A2, A3, A4, etc.

A reference such as A$1 will mean that row 1 is always referred to as you copy down the spreadsheet. If you were to copy across, the references would be updated to B1, C1, D1, etc.

A reference like A1 will mean that cell A1 is always referred to no matter what copying of the formula is carried out.

The **function key F4** adds dollar signs to the cell reference, cycling through one, two or zero dollar signs. Press the **F4** key as you are entering the cell address.

> If you haven't managed to create the outline explained above, open the spreadsheet called 'Cash flow exercise outline' (one of the spreadsheets you downloaded from www.bpp.com/aatspreadsheets).
>
> (1)   In cell B18 enter the formula =B6 (remember, it would be bad practice to enter 42,000 again: refer back to where it is first entered)
>
> (2)   In cell C18 enter the formula =B18*(1+$B7).
>
> (3)   Copy C18 across D18 to G18.

You should end up with the following figures:

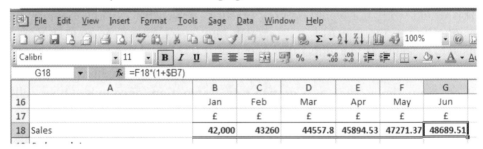

Note that the formula in G18 refers to cell F18 (the previous month's sales) but to cell B7 – the absolute address of the growth rate assumption.

The sales figures are untidy: some have comma separators between the thousands, some have one decimal place, some two. To tidy this up we will use **Format>Cells>** and choose the **Number** tab.

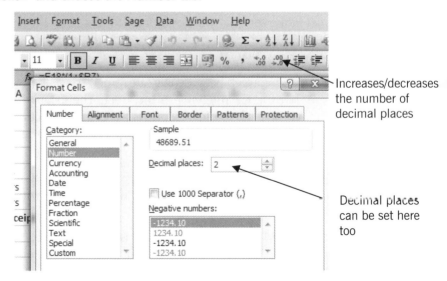

Increases/decreases the number of decimal places

Decimal places can be set here too

(1) Select the range of cells B18:G36.

(2) Click **Format>Format Cells**.

(3) Reduce the **Decimal places** to 0 and tick the **Use 1000 Separator (,)** check-box.

You should see that all the figures in your spreadsheet are now in the same format.

Now we'll concentrate on converting the sales to cash receipts, starting with cell C20. In February we will receive 60% of the sales made in January. Once again, be on your guard against inputting the same information repeatedly: refer to other cells where possible. Here the formula =B18*B9 would work, but as we are going to copy this across other months it will be important to make the reference to cell B9 absolute. Therefore, the formula you want is =B18*$B9.

(1) In cell C20 enter =B18*$B9

(2) Copy that across cells D20 to G20

(3) In cell D21 enter =B18*$B10

(4) Copy that across cells E21 to G21

(5) In cell E22 enter =B18*$B11

(6) Copy that across cells E22 to G22

(7) In cell B20 enter =B5*B9

(8) In cell B21 enter =$B5*$B10

(9) Copy B21 to C21

(10) In cell B22 enter =$B5*$B11

(11) Copy B22 across C22 and D22

(12) In cell B23 enter =Sum(B20:B22)

(13) Copy B23 across cells C23 to G23

(14) Format all the cells in the same way as we did for the **Sales** row

The top part of the cash flow spreadsheet should now be like this:

15	The cash flow						
16		Jan	Feb	Mar	Apr	May	Jun
17		£	£	£	£	£	£
18	Sales	42,000	43,260	44,558	45,895	47,271	48,690
19	Cash receipts						
20	1 month in arrears	27,000	25,200	25,956	26,735	27,537	28,363
21	2 months in arrears	13,500	13,500	12,600	12,978	13,367	13,768
22	3 months in arrears	3,150	3,150	3,150	2,940	3,028	3,119
23	Total operating receipts	43,650	41,850	41,706	42,653	43,932	45,250

And the formulae behind the cell contents should be:

15	The cash flow						
16		Jan	Feb	Mar	Apr	May	Jun
17		£	£	£	£	£	£
18	Sales	=B6	=B18*(1+$B7)	=C18*(1+$B7)	=D18*(1+$B7)	=E18*(1+$B7)	=F18*(1+$B7)
19	Cash receipts						
20	1 month in arrears	=B5*B9	=B18*$B9	=C18*$B9	=D18*$B9	=E18*$B9	=F18*$B9
21	2 months in arrears	=$B5*$B10	=$B5*$B10	=B18*$B10	=C18*$B10	=D18*$B10	=E18*$B10
22	3 months in arrears	=$B5*$B11	=$B5*$B11	=$B5*$B11	=B18*$B11	=C18*$B11	=D18*$B11
23	Total operating receipts	=SUM(B20:B22)	=SUM(C20:C22)	=SUM(D20:D22)	=SUM(E20:E22)	=SUM(F20:F22)	=SUM(G20:G22)

If your spreadsheet looks different from this, open the one called Cash Flow Exercise – Receipts (one of the spreadsheets you downloaded from www.bpp.com/aatspreadsheets).

Try to complete the spreadsheet, down to and including Total other payments.

You should not have to enter numbers anywhere. All your entries can be done by referencing other cells.

The spreadsheet should now look like:

15	The cash flow						
16		Jan	Feb	Mar	Apr	May	Jun
17		£	£	£	£	£	£
18	Sales	42,000	43,260	44,558	45,895	47,271	48,690
19	Cash receipts						
20	1 month in arrears	27,000	25,200	25,956	26,735	27,537	28,363
21	2 months in arrears	13,500	13,500	12,600	12,978	13,367	13,768
22	3 months in arrears	3,150	3,150	3,150	2,940	3,028	3,119
23	Total operating receipts	43,650	41,850	41,706	42,653	43,932	45,250
24							
25	Cash payments						
26	Purchases	27,300	28,119	28,963	29,831	30,726	31,648
27	Overheads	6,300	6,300	6,300	6,300	6,300	6,300
28	Total operating payments	33,600	34,419	35,263	36,131	37,026	37,948
29							
30	Dividends					10,000	
31	Capital purchases	3,600	12,600			1,800	
32	Total other payments	3,600	12,600	0	0	11,800	0

Finally, we get to the last three rows.

> (1) In Cell B34 enter the formula =B23-B28-B32.
>
> (2) Copy that across the remaining months.
>
> (3) In cell B35 enter =G8.
>
> (4) In cell B36 enter =B34+B35.
>
> (5) Copy that across the remaining months.
>
> (6) In cell C35 (the brought forward balance for February) enter =B36 (the carried forward balance from January.
>
> (7) Copy that across the remaining months.

The finished spreadsheet look like this:

	G36	▾	*fx* =G34+G35					
	A	B	C	D	E	F	G	H
1	Cash flow projection: six months January - June 20X6							
2								
3	Assumptions/variables							
4								
5	Historical monthly sales 20X5 (£)	45,000		Purchases = cost of sales.			65%	of sales
6	Projected sales Jan 20X6 (£)	42,000		Monthly overheads 20X5 (£)			6,000	
7	Monthly sales growth (2/X6 onwards)	3%		Rise in monthly overheads 20X6			5%	
8	Collection of debts:			Opening cash balance (O/d)			-7,500	
9	Month following sales	60%		Dividends (payable May 20X6, £)			10,000	
10	2nd month following sales	30%		Capital expenditure			18,000	
11	3rd month following sales	7%		Payable January			20%	
12	Uncollected	3%		Payable February			70%	
13				Payable May			10%	
14								
15	The cash flow							
16		Jan	Feb	Mar	Apr	May	Jun	
17		£	£	£	£	£	£	
18	Sales	42,000	43,260	44,558	45,895	47,271	48,690	
19	Cash receipts							
20	1 month in arrears	27,000	25,200	25,956	26,735	27,537	28,363	
21	2 months in arrears	13,500	13,500	12,600	12,978	13,367	13,768	
22	3 months in arrears	3,150	3,150	3,150	2,940	3,028	3,119	
23	Total operating receipts	43,650	41,850	41,706	42,653	43,932	45,250	
24								
25	Cash payments							
26	Purchases	27,300	28,119	28,963	29,831	30,726	31,648	
27	Overheads	6,300	6,300	6,300	6,300	6,300	6,300	
28	Total operating payments	33,600	34,419	35,263	36,131	37,026	37,948	
29								
30	Dividends					10,000		
31	Capital purchases	3,600	12,600			1,800		
32	Total other payments	3,600	12,600	0	0	11,800	0	
33								
34	Net cash flow	6,450	-5,169	6,443	6,521	-4,894	7,302	
35	Cash balance b/f	-7,500	-1,050	-6,219	224	6,746	1,852	
36	Cash balance c/f	-1,050	-6,219	224	6,746	1,852	9,154	

If your figures are different, you will find the above spreadsheet Cash Flow Exercise – Finished within the files downloaded from www.bpp.com/aatspreadsheets.

Tidy the spreadsheet up

The presentation is reasonable as we have taken care of it as we have developed the spreadsheet. This is good practice.

However, you may like to change **negative numbers** from being displayed with a **minus sign** to being displayed in **brackets**. This will require a special format. Depending on what your copy of Excel has been used for previously, that format may already exist, or you may have to create it.

To look for or create the cell format:

(1) Highlight the Cash Flow range B16:G36.

(2) Click on **Format>Cells>Number** and choose **Custom** from the bottom of the category list.

(3) Scroll down the **Type** list looking for a Type with the pattern: #,##0;(#,##0).

(4) The #,## indicates that a comma is to be used as the 000 separator.

(5) The 0 indicates no decimal places.

(6) #,##0 before the semicolon indicates format of positive numbers.

(7) (#,##0) after the semi-colon indicates format of negative numbers.

(8) If a suitable format is not found in the list, then create one by:

(9) Clicking on the format 0 (just after general).

(10) Type #,##0;(#,##0) or even better #,##0;[red](#,##0).

(11) Click OK.

(12) If you use the second suggestion, negative numbers will be in brackets **and** coloured red.

Other cell formatting options available from the same section of the toolbar include formatting as a particular currency or as a percentage.

Currency

Percentage

Take some time to play with these formatting options. Remember, you can always undo any action by pressing **Ctrl + Z**.

Add more information or explanation

It would be useful to know the basis or source of assumption and calculation methods. A simple way in which this can be documented is to use the Cell Comment facility.

Right click on cell B7 and choose **Insert comment** option for the list.

A box appears into which you can type your comment, such as:

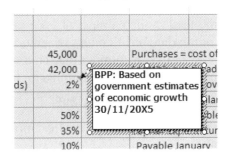

Press **Enter**.

A small red triangle is now visible at the top right off the cell indicating that it contains a comment. The comment appears if the cursor is placed on the cell.

Example: commission calculations

The following four telesales people each earn a basic salary of £14,000 pa. They also earn a commission of 2% of sales. The following spreadsheet has been created to process their commission and total earnings. Give an appropriate formula for each of the following cells.

(a) Cell D4
(b) Cell E6
(c) Cell D9
(d) Cell E9

	A	B	C	D	E
1	Sales team salaries and commissions - 200X				
2	Name	Sales	Salary	Commission	Total earnings
3		£	£	£	£
4	Northington	284,000	14,000	5,680	19,680
5	Souther	193,000	14,000	3,860	17,860
6	Weston	12,000	14,000	240	14,240
7	Easterman	152,000	14,000	3,040	17,040
8					
9	Total	641,000	56,000	12,820	68,820
10					
11					
12	Variables				
13	Basic Salary	14,000			
14	Commission rate	0.02			
15					

Solution

Possible formulae are:

(a)   =B4*B14

(b)   =C6+D6

(c)   =SUM(D4:D7)

(d)   There are a number of possibilities here, depending on whether you set the cell as the total of the earnings of each salesman (cells E4 to E7) or as the total of the different elements of remuneration (cells C9 and D9). Even better, would be a formula that checked that both calculations gave the same answer. A suitable formula for this purpose would be:

=IF(SUM(E4:E7)=SUM(C9:D9),SUM(E4:E7),"ERROR")

We explain this formula after the next example, don't worry about it at the moment!

Example: actual sales compared with budget sales

A business often compares its results against budgets or targets. It is useful to express differences or **variations as a percentage of the original budget**, for example sales may be 10% higher than predicted.

Continuing the telesales example, a spreadsheet could be set up as follows showing differences between actual sales and target sales, and expressing the difference as a percentage of target sales.

	A	B	C	D	E
1	Sales team comparison of actual against budget sales				
2	Name	Sales (Budget)	Sales (Actual)	Difference	% of budget
3		£	£	£	£
4	Northington	275,000	284,000	9,000	3.27
5	Souther	200,000	193,000	(7,000)	(3.50)
6	Weston	10,000	12,000	2,000	20.00
7	Easterman	153,000	152,000	(1,000)	(0.65)
8					
9	Total	638,000	641,000	3,000	0.47
10					

Give a suitable formula for each of the following cells.

(a)   Cell D4
(b)   Cell E6
(c)   Cell E9

Try this for yourself, before looking at the solution.

Solution

(a)   =C4 – B4

(b)   =(D6>B6)*100

(c)   =(D9>B9)*100. Note that in (c) you **cannot simply add up the individual percentage differences**, as the percentages are based on different quantities

FORMULAE WITH CONDITIONS

Suppose the employing company in the above example awards a bonus to people who exceed their target by more than £1,000. The spreadsheet could work out who is entitled to the bonus.

To do this we would enter the appropriate formula in cells F4 to F7. For salesperson Easterman, we would enter the following in cell F7:

=IF(D4>1000,"BONUS"," ")

We will now explain this **IF** formula.

IF statements follow the following structure (or syntax).

=IF(logical_test, value_if_true, value_if_false)

The logical_test is any value or expression that can be evaluated to Yes or No. For example, D4>1000 is a logical expression; if the value in cell D4 is over 1000, the expression evaluates to Yes. Otherwise, the expression evaluates to No.

Value_if_true is the value that is returned if the answer to the logical_test is Yes. For example, if the answer to D4>1000 is Yes, and the value_if_true is the text string "BONUS", then the cell containing the IF function will display the text "BONUS".

Value_if_false is the value that is returned if the answer to the logical_test is No. For example, if the value_if_false is two sets of quote marks "" this means display a blank cell if the answer to the logical test is No. So in our example, if D4 is not over 1000, then the cell containing the IF function will display a blank cell.

Note the following symbols which can be used in formulae with conditions:

<	less than
<=	less than or equal to
=	equal to
>=	greater than or equal to
>	greater than
<>	not equal to

Care is required to ensure **brackets** and **commas** are entered in the right places. If, when you try out this kind of formula, you get an error message, it may well be a simple mistake, such as leaving a comma out.

Using the IF function

A company offers a discount of 5% to customers who order more than £10,000 worth of goods. A spreadsheet showing what customers will pay may look like:

	C8	▼	f_x =IF(B8>C3, B8*C4,0)		
	A	B	C	D	E
1	Sales discount				
2					
3	Discount hurdle		10,000		
4	Discount rate		5%		
5					
6	Customer	Sales	Discount	Net price	
7		£	£	£	
8	John	12,000	600	11,400	
9	Margaret	9,000	0	9,000	
10	William	8,000	0	8,000	
11	Julie	20,000	1000	19,000	
12					

The formula in cell C8 is as shown: =IF(B8>C3, B8*C4, 0). This means, if the value in B8 is greater than £10,000 multiply it by the contents of C4, ie 5%, otherwise the discount will be zero. Cell D8 will calculate the amount net of discount, using the formula: =B8−C8. The same conditional formula with the cell references changed will be found in cells C9, C10 and C11.

Here is another example for you to try.

> Open the spreadsheet called Exam Results (one of the spreadsheets downloaded from www.bpp.com/aatspreadsheets).
>
> There are ten candidates listed together with their marks.
>
> The pass mark has been set at 50%
>
> See if you can complete column C rows 6–15 so that it shows PASS if the candidate scores 50 or above, and FAIL if the candidate scores less than 50.
>
> Once it's set up and working correctly, change the pass mark in cell B3 to 60 and ensure that the PASS>FAIL indications reflect the change.

The formulae you need will be based on the one for cell C6.

C6		▼		*fx* =IF(B6>B3,"Pass","Fail")	
	A	B	C	D	E
1	**Exam results**				
2					
3	Pass mark	50			
4					
5	**Candidate**	**Mark**	**Pass/fail**		
6	Alf	51	Pass		
7	Beth	56	Pass		
8	Charles	82	Pass		
9	David	42	Fail		
10	Edwina	68	Pass		
11	Frances	36	Fail		
12	Gary	75	Pass		
13	Hugh	53	Pass		
14	Iris	72	Pass		
15	John	34	Fail		

Conditional formatting

In addition to the condition determining whether PASS or FAIL appear, you can also conditionally format cell contents – for example, by altering the colour of a cell to highlight problems. This can be done by selecting **Format>Conditional Formatting**.

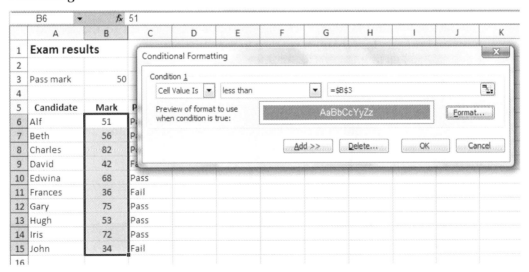

The marks which are less than the value in B3 have been highlighted by making the cell background red and the text white, as illustrated below:

	A	B	C
	J16	▾	f_x
1	**Exam results**		
2			
3	Pass mark	50	
4			
5	Candidate	Mark	Pass/fail
6	Alf	51	Pass
7	Beth	56	Pass
8	Charles	82	Pass
9	David	42	Fail
10	Edwina	68	Pass
11	Frances	36	Fail
12	Gary	75	Pass
13	Hugh	53	Pass
14	Iris	72	Pass
15	John	34	Fail
16			

To produce the above result:

Change the pass mark back to 50% if it is still at 60%.

Highlight the numbers in column B.

Click **Format>Conditional formatting**. For Condition 1 leave the first box as '**Cell Value Is**' then click the drop down arrow next to the second box and choose '**less than**'. Next click in the remaining box and type B3 (or click on that cell in the worksheet).

Then click on **Format>Patterns** and choose the red box. This changes the colour of the cell.

Then click on **Font** and click the down arrow next to '**Color**' and choose the white box.

Click **OK**.

CHARTS AND GRAPHS

Charts and graphs are useful and powerful ways of communicating trends and relative sizes of numerical data. Excel makes the production of charts relatively easy through the use of the chart wizard. The chart wizard is accessed either by **Insert>Chart**, or the chart button on the toolbar.

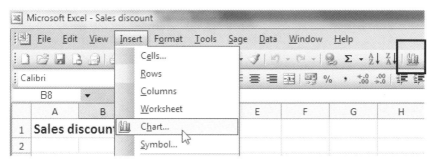

We will use the Sales discount spreadsheet, one of your downloaded files, to generate a number of different charts.

	A	B	C	D
	C8	▼	f_x =IF(B8>C3, B8*C4,0)	
1	Sales discount			
2				
3	Discount hurdle		10,000	
4	Discount rate		5%	
5				
6	Customer	Sales	Discount	Net price
7		£	£	£
8	John	12,000	600	11,400
9	Margaret	9,000	0	9,000
10	William	8,000	0	8,000
11	Julie	20,000	1000	19,000

First, we will generate a simple pie chart showing the total sales figure, before discounts.

A simple pie chart

(1) Open the Sales discount spreadsheet.

(2) Place you cursor on the word 'Customer' column, hold down the mouse button and drag the cursor downwards until you have selected the four names and four sales figures.

(3) Select **Insert>Chart** from the menu bar (or click the chart symbol) **Pie** and select the 3-D visual effect.

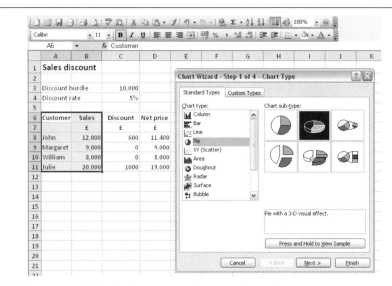

(4) Click **Next** and check the correct data is selected

(5) Click **Next** and change the **Chart title** to 'Sales for 20X6 (£)'

(6) Click **Next** and then **Finish**

This will generate a pie chart that looks like this:

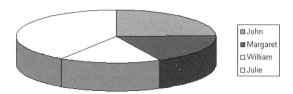

Resize the chart until you are happy with the layout.

You will see a Chart toolbar appear above your chart whenever you click in the chart area. This gives you a quick way to access a number of options, such as changing the chart type (see below).

Changing the chart type

If you decide that a different chart may be more suitable for presenting your data you can easily change the chart type.

---

(1) Click on your chart. From the menu bar click **Chart>Chart Type**, or click the drop down arrow next to the Chart Type button on the Chart toolbar.

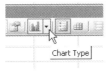

(2) From here, pick some charts from the following chart types to see what they produce: **Bar**, **Bubble**, **Doughnut** and **Line**. For example the doughnut chart will produce something like this:

Sales for 20X6 (£)

☑ John
■ Margaret
☐ William
☐ Julie

Bar charts

A pie chart is good for showing relative sizes of elements making up a total. However, sometimes you may want to be able to compare how two series of data are moving: sales and gross profit for example. In this case, bar charts (or line charts) are more suitable.

Excel makes a distinction between bar charts that show vertical bars and those that show horizontal bars. When the data is shown vertically Excel refers to the chart as a 'column' chart whereas if the data is shown horizontally it is a 'bar' chart.

We are going to create a column chart showing the Sales and Net Price figure from the data on the Sales Discount spreadsheet.

---

(1) Delete your chart by clicking on its outer most frame and pressing the **Delete** key.

(2) Place the cursor on the word 'Customer' and drag the cursor down until all four names have been selected.

> (3) Hold down the Ctrl button and select B6:B11. Still holding the Ctrl button down, select D8:D11.
>
> (4) Release the mouse button and Ctrl key.
>
> (5) Choose **Clustered column with a 3-D visual effect** from the chart types.

The Chart Wizard now shows:

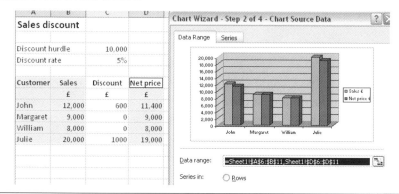

> (1) Click on the **Series** tab
>
> (2) You will see that the chart has automatically picked up the **Series** (or 'legend' names) from rows 6 and 7. If you are happy with these click **Next**. If not, click on a series name, then either type in the name you want, for example 'Sales', or click on the chart icon at the end of the **Name** box and choose the cell with the name you want (here it would be B6). Now click the other series name and choose a name for that, for example 'Net price', or choose cell D6, then Click **Next**
>
> (3) This time there is no automatic chart title so we will need to add one on the **Titles** tab, so type "Sales and Net Prices for 20X6 (£)".

You should also label the horizontal axis and the vertical axis. This is also done from the Titles tab.

> (1) To label the horizontal axis, click in the **Category (X) Axis** box and type 'Customer'
>
> (2) To label the other axis, click in the **Category (Z) Axis** box and type a pound sign.
>
> (3) Click Finish.

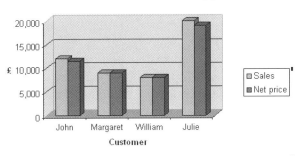

Sales and Net Sales for 20X6 (£)

Note that if you are typing words for the vertical axis title you can change the direction of the text by clicking on the **Format Axis** button on the **Chart** toolbar, then clicking **Alignment** and changing the **Orientation**. Try experimenting with that now.

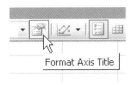

Format Axis Title

Formatting existing charts

Even after your chart is 'finished' you can change it in a variety of ways by using the options available in **Chart>Chart Options**. In addition:

(a) You can **resize it** simply by selecting it and dragging out one of its corners.

(b) You can change the scale by dragging out the top, base or sides. To do so, hover your cursor over any of the black squares around the frame of the chart until your cursor turns into a **double ended arrow**. Drag with the mouse button still held down.

(c) You can change **each element** by **double clicking** on it then selecting from the options available.

(d) You can also select any item of text and alter the wording. You can also change the size, font or **colours** using the usual buttons on the **Formatting** toolbar.

PRINTING, LINKING AND EMBEDDING

Printing spreadsheets

The print options for your spreadsheet may be accessed by selecting **File>Print>OK** or pressing **Ctrl + P**. Printing large spreadsheets without checking the print and layout settings will often result in printouts spread messily over several pages.

It is a good idea to at least opt for **File>Print Preview** to see what your printout will look like before printing. You can also access this option by pressing the **Print Preview** icon on the standard toolbar.

A better option is to control what prints more precisely, and for example, to print out selected areas only, include/exclude gridlines and the column and row headings, alter the orientation of the page etc.

Open the spreadsheet we saw earlier called Cash Flow Exercise – Finished.

Assume that we only want to print out the cash flow without the table at the top showing the assumptions.

We want to show the gridlines but not the A, B, C… or 1, 2, 3… that head up columns and rows.

(1)   Select the range A15:G36

(2)   Choose **File>Print Area>Set Print Area**

(3)   Check the **Gridlines** box in **File>Page Setup** in the **Sheet** tab

(4)   Choose **File>Print Preview**

The printout will stretch over two pages, with just the June figures on the second page. This is clearly unsatisfactory.

Close the **Print Preview** window.

Looking back at the Cash Flow spreadsheet, you will see a double dotted line round the print area selected, but between May and June there is a single dotted line indicating where Excel automatically made the unfortunate page break.

The easiest way to solve this problem is:

(1)   Choose **File>Page Setup**

(2)   Choose the **Page** tab

(3)   Under **Scaling**, choose **Fit to 1 page**.

You will see the page break line disappears and a Print Preview will show the selected areas all on one page.

At this point you can check for obvious layout and formatting errors.

If you have a printer attached you might want to print out the selected area now.

Spelling

Before you print it is also wise to check your work for spelling mistakes. To do this click **Tools** on the menu bar and select **Spelling**. If you have made any spelling errors Excel will offer alternative **Suggestions** which you can accept by clicking **Change** or ignore by clicking **Ignore** (**Once** or **All**).

If the word is in fact correct (for example, terminology that Excel does not recognise) you can add it to Excel's dictionary by clicking **Add to Dictionary**.

Preparing your spreadsheet for printing: Page set-up

The **Page Setup** options allow you to specify certain other details that affect how your spreadsheet looks when it prints out.

Imagine you are printing out a spreadsheet that will cover several pages. It is important that certain information is present on each page. For example:

- The spreadsheet title
- The page number and total pages
- The author
- The row and column headings

The **File>Page Setup, Header/Footer** and **Sheet** tabs allows you to specify this information.

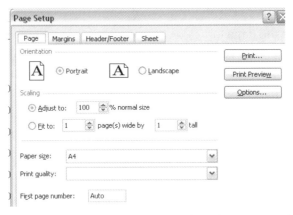

From here you can set the size of the **Margins** (the white spaces that print around the spreadsheet) and choose whether to print the spreadsheet in **Landscape Orientation** (ie wider than tall) rather than the default portrait **Orientation** (taller than wide) from the **Page** tab.

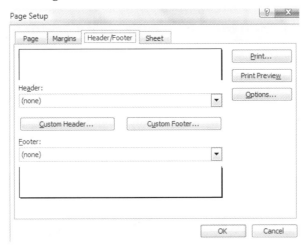

Headers appear at the top of each page. For example, a customer header could be:

Author   Budget for 2012   Date printed

Footers appear at the bottom of each page, for example:

Page   File name

The **Sheet** tab allows you to specify the rows and columns to be repeated on each page. For example, you might want to repeat the months across the top of each page and the type of income down the left of each page.

We have provided a demonstration spreadsheet in the downloaded files Print practice. Open it, and try the following:

> Insert a **Header**: Author name, Title (Budget 2012) Date printed

> Insert a **Footer**: Page number, File name

(use the custom Header/Footer options for these)

Ensure that the headings in column A are repeated on the second page.

You can also use this spreadsheet to experiment with page breaks (**Print Preview>View page break preview** or **View>Page break preview**, then move the blue dotted lines to where you want the page break(s)) and any other **Page Setup** options.

Printing formulae

Occasionally, perhaps for documentation or checking, you might want the spreadsheet formulae to be printed out instead of the calculated results of the formula. To do this:

(1) Display the formulae on the screen by **Tools>Options>Show formulas**

(2) Set the area you want to be printed **Page Layout>Print Area>Set Area**

(3) Check what the printout will look like **File>Print preview**

(4) Adjust as necessary and print out when happy with the display

Printing charts

Charts can be printed either with or without the data on the worksheet.

To print only the chart simply click on it and then press **Ctrl + P**. As always, it is wise to **Print Preview** first.

If you also want to print the worksheet data, click away from the chart into any cell. Use **Print Preview** to make sure that the chart is the right size and is in the right position. Then press **Ctrl + P**.

USING SPREADSHEETS WITH WORD PROCESSING SOFTWARE

There may be a situation where you wish to incorporate the contents of all or part of a spreadsheet into a **word processed report**. There are a number of options available to achieve this.

(a) The simplest, but least flexible option, is to **print out** the spreadsheet and interleave the page or pages at the appropriate point in your word processed document.

(b) A neater option if you are just including a small table is to select and **copy** the relevant cells from the spreadsheet to the computer's clipboard by selecting the cells and Pressing **Ctrl+C** (or using the **Copy** button from the formatting toolbar). Then switch to the word processing document, and **Paste** them in (for example, by using **Ctrl+V**) at the appropriate point. The pasted material is now completely separate from its source spreadsheet. If the spreadsheet is changed, the copied and pasted material will not change, and you have to go through the copy>paste procedure again to update the report.

(c) Office packages, such as Microsoft Office allow you to **link** spreadsheets and word processing files.

For example, a new, blank spreadsheet can be '**embedded**' in a document by selecting **Insert> Object** then, from within the Create New tab, selecting **Microsoft Office Excel Worksheet**. The spreadsheet is then available to be worked upon, allowing the easy manipulation of numbers using all the facilities of the spreadsheet package. Clicking outside the spreadsheet will result in the spreadsheet being inserted into the document.

The contents of an existing spreadsheet may be inserted into a Word document by choosing **Insert>Object** and then activating the **Create from File** tab. Then click the **Browse** button and locate the spreadsheet file. Highlight the file, then click Insert, ensure you click the box next to the **Link to File** option, and then **OK**. You may then need to move and resize the object, by dragging its borders, to fit your document.

Provided Automatic update has been activated in the Word file, the linked object will be updated every time you open the file that contains the object or any time the linked object changes while the file is open.

(1) Open the downloaded spreadsheet called Linking Experiment.

(2) Save this to a location you will remember, for example, the desktop:

File>Save as>Desktop>Linking experiment

(3) Keep Excel open, but now open Word and create a new document.

(4) In Word click **Insert>Object>Create from file** and browse to find the Linking Experiment file you just saved.

(5) Ensure the '**Link to File**' box is checked.

(6) Click **OK**.

You will see the Linking Experiment appear in the Word document.

(7) Keep the Word file open, but switch back to the Excel and the open Linking Experiment spreadsheet.

(8) Change the top figure to 15 (the total will change to 43).

(9) Look again at the Word file and you will see that it has also been changed in line with the linked spreadsheet.

You can close the file without saving as you won't need them again.

Importing data to Excel

You may wish to include data in a spreadsheet that comes from, say, a Microsoft Word document, a PowerPoint Presentation or another spreadsheet.

The easiest way to do this is select the text you wish to include, click the **Copy** button (or press **Ctrl + C**).

Open the spreadsheet that you wish to use the data in if it is not already open and click the **Paste** button (or press **Ctrl + V**).

CHAPTER OVERVIEW

- A **spreadsheet** is basically an electronic piece of paper divided into **rows** and **columns**. The intersection of a row and a column is known as a **cell**.

- Essential basic **skills** include how to **move around** within a spreadsheet, how to **enter** and **edit** data, how to **fill** cells, how to **insert** and **delete** columns and rows and how to improve the basic **layout** and **appearance** of a spreadsheet.

- **Relative** cell references (eg B3) change when you copy formulae to other locations or move data from one place to another. **Absolute** cell references (eg B3) stay the same.

- A wide range of **formulae** and functions are available within Excel. We looked at the use of conditional formulae that use an **IF** statement.

- A spreadsheet should be given a **title** which clearly defines its purpose. The contents of rows and columns should also be clearly **labelled**. **Formatting** should be used to make the data in the spreadsheet easy to read and interpret.

- **Numbers** can be **formatted** in several ways, for instance with commas, as percentages, as currency or with a certain number of decimal places.

- Excel includes the facility to produce a range of charts and graphs. The **Chart Wizard** provides a tool to simplify the process of chart construction.

- Spreadsheets can be **linked** to, and exchange data with, **word processing documents** – and *vice versa*.

- Spreadsheets can be used in a variety of accounting contexts. You should practise using spreadsheets, **hands-on experience** is the key to spreadsheet proficiency.

TEST YOUR LEARNING

Test 1

List three types of cell contents.

Test 2

What do the F5 and F2 keys do in Excel?

Test 3

What technique can you use to insert a logical series of data such as 1, 2 .... 10, or Jan, Feb, March etc?

Test 4

How do you display formulae instead of the results of formulae in a spreadsheet?

Test 5

List five possible changes that may improve the appearance of a spreadsheet.

Test 6

What is the syntax (pattern) of an IF function in Excel?

Test 7

The following spreadsheet shows sales of two products, the Ego and the Id, for the period July to September.

	A	B	C	D	E
1	Sigmund Ltd				
2	Sales analysis - quarter 3, 2010				
3		July	August	September	Total
4	Ego	3,000	4,000	2,000	9,000
5	Id	2,000	1,500	4,000	7,500
6	Total	5,000	5,500	6,000	16,500

Devise a suitable formula for each of the following cells.

(a) Cell B6
(b) Cell E5
(c) Cell E6

Test 8

The following spreadsheet shows sales, exclusive of VAT, the VAT amounts and the VAT inclusive amounts. There is a strong possibility that the VAT rate of 17.5% will change soon so it is important to construct the spreadsheet so that it can easily be adapted.

	A	B	C	D
1	Taxable Supplies Ltd		Vat rate	0.175
2				
3		January	February	March
4	Product A	5,000	4,000	3,000
5	Product B	2,000	1,500	4,000
6	Product C	7,000	5,700	4,000
7	Product D	2,000	3,000	1,000
8	Product E	1,000	2,400	6,000
9	Total net	17,000	16,600	18,000
10	VAT	2,975	2,905	3,150
11	Total gross	19,975	19,505	21,150

Suggest suitable formulae for cells:

(a)   B9
(b)   C10
(c)   D11

chapter 4:
MORE ADVANCED SPREADSHEET TECHNIQUES (EXCEL 2003)

─────── **chapter coverage** 📖 ───────

In this chapter we explore some of the more advanced aspects of spreadsheets using Excel 2003.

This chapter covers:

- ✐ The importance of regularly saving and backing up spreadsheets.

- ✐ Controlling access to spreadsheets, including making spreadsheets available for sharing.

- ✐ Checking the validity of data when entering it into a spreadsheet.

- ✐ Working with multiple worksheets that refer to each other.

- ✐ Sophisticated data handling including sorting, filtering, pivot tables and look-up tables.

- ✐ Statistical tools and functions that help in analysing data.

- ✐ Using combination charts to compare two sets of unrelated data on the same chart.

- ✐ Error detection and prevention.

CONTROLS, SECURITY AND SHARING

Back-ups, passwords and cell protection

There are facilities available in spreadsheet packages which can be used as controls – to prevent unauthorised or accidental amendment or deletion of all or part of a spreadsheet. There are also facilities available for hiding data, and for preventing (or alerting) users about incorrect data.

Saving files and backing up

(a) **Saving**. When working on a spreadsheet, save your file regularly, as often as every ten minutes using **File>Save**, **Ctrl + S** or the **Save** button on the standard toolbar.

This will prevent too much work being lost in the advent of a system crash.

Save files in the appropriate **folder** so that they are easy to locate. If you need to save the file to a new folder, select the '**New folder**' option after clicking **File>Save**. Where this option is located depends on the operating system you are using. For example, in Windows 7, you simply click the **New folder** button; in Windows XP click the new folder icon.

Give the folder a suitable name (for example, the name of the client you are working on or following your employer's standard naming practice).

(b) **Save as**. A simple save overwrites the existing file. If you use **Save as** then you can give the file a different name, preserving previous versions. For example Save as "Budget Edition 1", Budget Edition 2", Budget Edition 3". This is much safer than simply relying on the most recent version – which might be beyond fixing!

(c) **Back-ups.** Because data and the computers or storage devices on which it is stored can easily be lost or destroyed, it is vital to take regular copies or back-ups. If the data is lost, the back-up copy can be used to **restore** the data up to the time the back-up was taken. Spreadsheet files should be included in standard backup procedures, for example the daily back-up routine.

The back-ups could be held on a separate external hard drive, or perhaps a USB memory stick, and should stored away from the original data, in case there is a fire or other disaster at the organisation's premises. Alternatively the back-ups can be saved to a network location. Some back-ups are now stored on the Internet.

(d) **AutoRecover.** Excel has a built-in feature that saves copies of all open Excel files at a fixed time interval. The files can be restored if Excel closes unexpectedly, such as during a power failure.

> (1) Turn on the **AutoRecover** feature by clicking **Tools>Options**
>
> (2) Click the **Save** tab
>
> (3) Check **Save Autorecover info every…**
>
> (4) Choose the time interval. The default time between saves is every 10 minutes. To change this, enter any number of minutes between 1 and 120
>
> In the **AutoRecover save location** box, you can type the path and the folder name of the location in which you want to keep the AutoRecover files.

Protection

(a) **Cell protection/cell locking**. This prevents the user from inadvertently changing cells that should not be changed. There are two ways of specifying which cells should be protected:

(i) All cells are locked except those specifically unlocked. This method is useful when you want most cells to be locked. When protection is implemented, all cells are locked unless they have previously been excluded from the protection process. You will also see here a similar mechanism for hiding data.

> Once again, open the spreadsheet Cash Flow Exercise–Finished.
>
> Highlight the range B5:B12. This contains some of the assumptions on which the cash flow forecast is based and this is the only range of cells that we want to be unlocked and available for alteration.
>
> (1) Choose **Format>Cells>Protection**

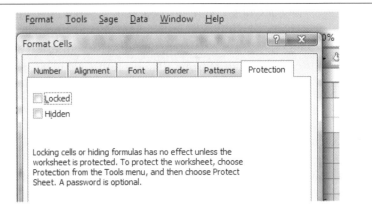

(2) Untick the **Locked** and **Hidden** boxes

(3) Click on **OK**

(4) Now go to the **Tools>Protection>Protect Sheet**

(5) Click on **Protect Sheet**

Don't enter a password when prompted, simply click **OK**.

Now investigate what you can change on the spreadsheet. You should find that only cells B5:B12 can be changed. If you try to change anything else a message comes up telling you that the cell is protected.

Click on **Tools>Protection>Unprotect Sheet** to make every cell accessible to change again.

(ii) Most are unlocked, except those specified as being locked. This method is useful if only a few cells have to be locked.

(1) Open the spreadsheet Sales discount.

(2) Assume that we want to lock only the 10,000 in cell C3 and the 5% figure in cell C4.

(3) Select the whole worksheet (click on top left-hand square between 1 and A)

(4) Untick the **Locked** and **Hidden** boxes

(5) Click on **OK** (this stops everything from being locked)

(6) Select cells C3 and C4

(7) Tick the **Locked** and **Hidden** boxes

(8) To implement the lock you then have to click on **Protect Sheet** from the same drop-down menu. The cells can still be changed if you do not do this step.

> (9)   You are offered the chance to enter a password
>
> Now you will be prevented from changing just those two cells.

(b)   **Passwords**. All access to the spreadsheet can be protected and the spreadsheet encrypted or password protected from amendment but it can, however, be seen without a password. This can be done by:

(1)   **File>Save as**

(2)   **Tools>General options**

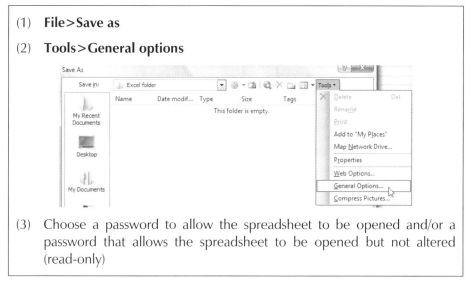

(3)   Choose a password to allow the spreadsheet to be opened and/or a password that allows the spreadsheet to be opened but not altered (read-only)

Now, if you close the file and re-open it, you will be asked for a password to get full access, or without the password you can open it in read-only mode so that it can be seen but not altered.

Sharing workbooks

It is possible to share a workbook with colleagues so that the same file can be viewed by more than one person at a time. This can be done in a number of ways.

Send as an attachment

One way to share a spreadsheet with colleagues is to send it as an attachment in an email. If your computer is set up with a mail client such as Microsoft Outlook you can click **File>Send To>Mail Recipient** to quickly send the spreadsheet you are working on as an attachment.

Alternatively you can first draft the email and attach the spreadsheet using your email program's options and the Windows Explorer menu.

However, if each recipient of the email makes changes to the document, this will lead to the existence of a number of different versions of the same document, and a potential loss of version control (see above). This is not, therefore, a recommended method of sharing spreadsheets.

Save to a shared network server

Another way to make a spreadsheet available to colleagues is to save it in a place on the network server that is also accessible to them. Anyone with access to that particular location will be able to open the file but, if more than one person tries to open the file, only the first person will be able to make changes to it. Anyone else subsequently opening the file will only be able to open a 'Read Only' version of it, so they will be able to view the contents but not make any changes.

This method prevents loss of version control but is not particularly useful if other people wish to make changes at the same time.

Share workbook method

A more practical method is to use the inbuilt sharing function in Excel. This allows different people to open and make changes to the same document at the same time, and for these changes to be tracked.

Click **Tools>Share Workbook**. Click the **Editing** tab and select **Allow changes by more than one user at the same time**. From here you can also see who has the document open.

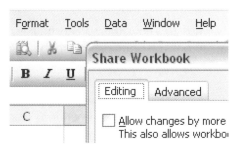

Other settings are available from the **Advanced** tab such as choosing how long to keep the change history for, how frequently to update changes and what to do if users make conflicting changes.

To stop any tracked changes from being lost click **File>Tools>Protection>Protect Share Workbook** and click **Sharing with track changes**. This option also allows you to set a password so only those with the password can make changes.

Data validation

Sometimes only a specific type or range of data is valid for a certain cell or cells. For example, if inputting hours worked in a week from a time sheet it could be known that no one should have worked more than 60 hours. It is possible to test data as it is input and to either prevent input completely or simply warn that the input value looks odd. This is known as 'data validation' or 'data restriction'.

C2	▼	f_x =A2*B2	
	A	B	C
1	Hours	Rate/hr	Pay
2	10	7	70

In this simple spreadsheet, C2 holds the only formula; A2 and B2 are cells into which data will be entered, but we want the data to conform to certain rules:

Hours <= 60. If greater than 60, a warning is to be issued. Rate>hr >=8 and <=20. Data outside that range should be rejected.

(1) Set up a new spreadsheet with the above data and make A2 the active cell. Go to **Data>Validation**.

(2) Under the **Data Validation Settings** tab, select **Allow Decimal**, then select **less than or equal to** from the drop-down **Data** list and enter 60 as the **Maximum**.

(3) Under the **Input Message** tab enter '**Warning**' as the title and '**Hours expected to be less than 60**' as the input message.

(4) Under the **Error Alert** tab change the **Style** to **Warning**, enter '**Attention**' as the title and 'Check hours: look too large' as the Error message.

(5) Click **OK**.

(6) Now try to enter, say 70 into A2. You will first see an information message explaining the data that is expected, then a warning message and the option to continue.

(7) Now try to set up cell B2 with appropriate messages and to prevent any value outside the range 8–20 from being entered at all.

THREE DIMENSIONAL (MULTI-SHEET) SPREADSHEETS

Background

In early spreadsheet packages, a spreadsheet file consisted of a single worksheet. As mentioned earlier, Excel provides the option of multi-sheet spreadsheets, consisting of a series of related sheets.

For example, suppose you were producing a profit forecast for two regions, and a combined forecast for the total of the regions. This situation would be suited to using separate worksheets for each region and another for the total. This approach is sometimes referred to as working in **three dimensions**, as you are able to flip between different sheets stacked in front or behind each other. Cells in one sheet may **refer** to cells in another sheet. So, in our example, the formulae in the cells in the total sheet would refer to the cells in the other sheets.

Excel has a series of 'tabs', one for each worksheet at the bottom of the spreadsheet.

How many worksheets?

Excel can be set up so that it always opens a fresh file with a certain number of worksheets ready and waiting for you. Click on **Tools>Options>General** and set the number of '**Sheets in new workbook**' to the number you would like each workbook to contain to contain (sheets may be added or deleted later).

If you subsequently want to insert more sheets use **Insert>Worksheet**.

By default sheets are called Sheet 1, Sheet 2 etc. However, these may be changed. To rename a sheet in Excel, right click on its index tab and choose the **Rename** option. You can drag the sheets into different orders by clicking on the tab, holding down the mouse button and dragging a sheet to its new position.

Pasting from one sheet to another

When building a spreadsheet that will contain a number of worksheets with identical structure, users often set up one sheet, then copy that sheet and amend its contents.

To copy a worksheet in Excel, from within the worksheet you wish to copy, select **Home>Cells>Format>Move or Copy sheet** (or right click the worksheet tab and select **Move or Copy)** and tick the **Create a copy** box.

A 'Total' sheet would use the same structure, but would contain formulae totalling the individual sheets.

Linking sheets with formulae

Formulae on one sheet may refer to data held on another sheet. The links within such a formula may be established using the following steps.

Step 1   In the cell that you want to refer to a cell from another sheet, type =.

Step 2   Click on the index tab for the sheet containing the cell you want to refer to and select the cell in question.

Step 3   Press Enter.

---

(1)   Open the spreadsheet called 3D spreadsheet example.

This consists of three worksheets. The Branch A and Branch B sheets hold simple trading and profit and loss accounts. There are both numbers and formulae in those sheets. The Company sheet contains only headings, but is set out in the same pattern as the two branch sheets.

We want to combine the Branch figures onto the Company sheet.

(2)   On the company sheet, make D2 the active cell

(3)   Enter =

(4)   Click on Branch A and click on D2

(5)   Enter +

(6)   Click on Branch B and click on D2

(7)   Press Enter

You will see that the formula ='Branch A'!D2+'Branch B'!D2 is now in cell D2 of the Company sheet and that the number displayed is 500,000, the sum of the sales in each branch.

In the company sheet, copy D2 (**Ctrl+C**) and paste (**Ctrl+V**) to D3, D4, C6, C7, C8, and D9 to complete the profit and loss account.

The company sheet will now look like this:

	A	B	C	D
				='Branch A'!D9+'Branch B'!D9
1	Company		£	£
2	Sales			500,000
3	Cost of sales			270,000
4	Gross profit			230,000
5	Expenses:			
6	Selling and distribution		70,000	
7	Administration		45,000	
8				115,000
9	Net profit			115,000
10				

D9 cell reference, formula: ='Branch A'!D9+'Branch B'!D9

This is arithmetically correct, but needs lines>rules to format it correctly.

Use **Format>Cells>Borders** to insert appropriate single and double lines/rules in the cells:

The final consolidated results should look like:

G17 cell reference

	A	B	C	D
1	Company		£	£
2	Sales			500,000
3	Cost of sales			270,000
4	Gross profit			230,000
5	Expenses:			
6	Selling and distribution		70,000	
7	Administration		45,000	
8				115,000
9	Net profit			115,000

Note that if you change any figures in Branch A or Branch B, the figures will also change on the company spreadsheet.

Uses for multi-sheet spreadsheets

There are a wide range of situations suited to the multi-sheet approach. A variety of possible uses follow.

(a) A spreadsheet could use one sheet for variables, a second for calculations, and a third for outputs.

(b) To enable quick and easy **consolidation** of similar sets of data, for example the financial results of two subsidiaries or the budgets of two departments.

(c) To provide different views of the same data. For instance, you could have one sheet of data sorted into product code order and another sorted into product name order.

DATA MANIPULATION

Data manipulation refers to a number of techniques available in Excel for summarising, analysing, sorting and presenting data.

Simple data manipulation

A database can be viewed simply as a collection of data. There is a simple 'database' spreadsheet related to inventory, called Stockman Ltd in your downloaded files. **Open it now**.

There are a number of features worth pointing out in this spreadsheet before we start data manipulation.

(1) Each row from 4–15 holds an inventory record.

(2) Column G makes use of the **IF** function to determine if the inventory needs to be reordered (when quantity < reorder level).

(3) In row 2 the spreadsheet uses automatic word wrap within some cells. This can improve presentation if there are long descriptions.

To use word wrap:

(1) Select the cells you want to format

(2) **Format>Cells>Alignment**

(3) Under **Text Control** select **Wrap Text**

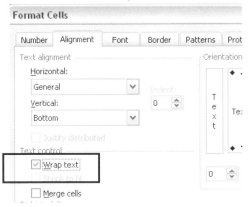

If all wrapped text is not visible, the row may be set to a specific height. Select **Format>Row>Autofit**.

The data is currently arranged in part number order.

The horizontal rows are records: one record for each inventory type. The vertical columns are attributes (qualities) relating to each record.

Sorting the data

Let's say that we want to sort the data into descending value order.

---

(1) Select the data range A4:G15

(2) Select **Data>Sort**

> (3) Choose to sort by column F, descending
>
> (4) Click **OK**

You will see that the data has been sorted by value.

If you now **Sort by** Supplier (**Ascending**) you will have the data arranged by supplier, and within that by value.

Filtering the data

Filtering data allows you to select and display just some of it in the table. This is very useful if the table consists of many records and you just need to find some of them.

> Sort the data back into Part code order.
>
> Let's say we just want to find inventory records relating to suppliers B and C.
>
> (1) Select **Data > Filter > Autofilter**
>
> (2) Click on the drop-down arrow that has appeared at the top of the Supplier column
>
> (3) Select **Custom** then complete the dialogues as follows:

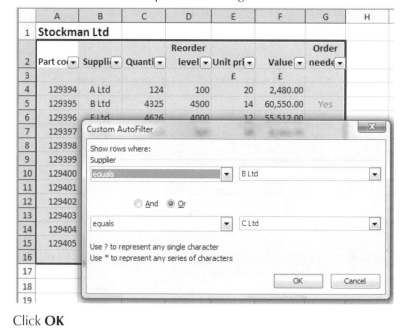

> Click **OK**

Only the records relating to suppliers B and C are visible and these can be manipulated (eg sorted) as an independent subset of the whole table.

Note that the other records are still there and are included in the total value figure. It's simply that they have been obscured for presentation.

You will also see a little funnel symbol at the top of the Supplier column informing that there is filtering in place on this attribute.

Make all the records visible again by removing the filter:

(1)   Click the drop-down arrow in the Supplier column

(2)   Select *(All)*

(3)   Click *OK*

(4)   Sort the data back into Part code order if it's not already in that order

(5)   To get rid of the little filter arrows, untick **AutoFilter** in **Data>Filter**

Find and replace

Let's now say that that Supplier A Ltd has been taken over and that its name has changed to Acorn plc.

(1)   Click on **Edit>Find**

(2)   Select the **Find** tab

(3)   Enter A Ltd in the **Find what:** box

(4)   Click on the Replace tab and enter Acorn Plc in the **Replace with:** box

(5)   Click on **Replace All**

Note. You could instead click on **Edit>Replace** (or press **Ctrl + H**) as a shortcut.

You should see that all occurrences of A Ltd have been replaced by Acorn plc.

If no range is specified before this step then the whole spreadsheet would be affected. If a range is specified, the search and replace occurs only within that range.

Σ AutoSum

You have already used **Σ** (sometimes called **AutoSum**) as a way of specifying a range of data to add up. However, the **Σ AutoSum** drop-down list also contains other useful functions such as:

- **Average**
- **Count numbers**
- **Maximum**
- **Minimum**

Still using the Stockman Ltd spreadsheet:

(1)   Select cells E4...E15

(2)   From the **Σ** drop-down list on the standard toolbar select **Max**

> You will see 65 appear in cell E16 (just below the last unit price). The formula in that cell is =MAX(E4:E15).
>
> Try some of the other Σ functions.

The results given by the Σ functions are always just under a column of data, or immediately to the right of a row of data.

If you want the results to appear in a different cell, you have to type the appropriate formula into that cell. For example, typing =MAX(E4:E15) into cell A20 will show the maximum unit price of the inventory in cell A20.

Pivot tables

Pivot tables are a very powerful way of analysing data. Look at the following simple example relating to sales by a music company.

	A	B	C
1	Sales data		
2			
3	Customer	Source	Amount spent (£)
4	Bill	CDs	50
5	Chris	Vinyl	10
6	Sandra	Merchandise	30
7	Graham	CDs	45
8	Chris	Merchandise	20
9	Chris	Vinyl	10
10	Chris	CDs	10
11	Caroline	Merchandise	30
12	Graham	Tickets	75
13	Fred	Vinyl	30
14	Bill	CDs	20
15	Graham	CDs	60
16	Chris	Vinyl	10
17	Sandra	Tickets	50
18	Bill	Tickets	26
19	Caroline	Vinyl	24
20			
21		Total	£500

The information has simply been listed and totalled on the spreadsheet. It would be useful to be able to show:

- Sales per customer
- Sales by source

Ideally, we would like to produce a table which displays sales by both source and by customer: this type of table is called a pivot table.

(1) Open the spreadsheet file called Pivot table example which contains the above data.

(2) Select the range A4:C19

(3) Select **Data>PivotTable and PivotChart Report**

(4) Select the **Microsoft Office Excel list or Database** radio button

(5) Select the **PivotTable** radio button

(6) Click **Next**

(7) Accept the range offered and click on **Next**

(8) Select **Existing worksheet** and enter E4 as the location

(9) Click **Finish**

The PivotTable Field List window opens

(10) Drag Source into **Row Fields**, Customer into **Column Fields** and Amount spent (£) into the **Data space**

The pivot table is now transformed into the two-dimensional table we want.

(11) Tidy it up a little by selecting F5 to L5 and right justifying these names by clicking on the appropriate alignment button on the toolbar

Note the two drop down arrows on the pivot table that allow filtering of the data.

Sum of Amount spent (£)	Customer ▼						
Source ▼		Bill	Caroline	Chris	Fred	Graham	Sandra	Grand Total
CDs		70		10		105		185
Merchandise			30	20			30	80
Tickets		26				75	50	151
Vinyl			24	30	30			84
Grand Total		96	54	60	30	180	80	500

If you had difficulty with this, the spreadsheet called 'Pivot table result Excel 2003' is available within your downloaded files.

Experiment with different settings. Clicking on the pivot table will bring up the **PivotTable Field List** window again if it has disappeared.

Note that if the original data is altered, the pivot table does *not* change until you right-click on it and select **Refresh** from the list of options.

Look-up tables

The Look-up function allows you to find and use data that is held in a table. Here is a simple example:

	A	B	C	D	E	F	G	H	I
1	**Salesman Ltd**								
2	Part code	VATcode	Unit price		VAT rate	17.500%			
3			£						
4	129394	1	20.00						
5	129395	1	14.00		Invoice				
6	129396	0	12.00						
7	129397	0	14.00						
8	129398	1	37.00		*Part code*	*Quantity*	*Unit price*	*VAT*	£
9	129399	0	65.00		129396	10	12.00	0	120.00
10	129400	1	34.00					Net	120.00
11	129401	0	20.00					VAT	0.00
12	129402	1	10.00					Total	120.00
13	129403	0	34.00						
14	129404	0	25.00						
15	129405	1	35.00						
16									

On the left is a price list. If a part has a VAT code of 1, then VAT will be charged at the rate as set in cell F2; if the VAT code is 0, then no VAT is chargeable.

To create this invoice, you would look down the part numbers column, until you found 129396. You would then read across to find the unit price and VAT code and, together with the quantity sold, you could create the invoice.

This process has been automated in the spreadsheet Salesman Ltd that is on your CD.

(1)   Open the Spreadsheet called Salesman Ltd.

(2)   Click on cell G9 to reveal the use of the VLOOKUP function.

Cell G9 holds the formula =VLOOKUP(E9,A4:C15,3, FALSE)

This means: look for the value held in cell E9, in the first row of the range A4:C15, and return the value in the third column of the range: it will return the price relating to the part number. FALSE (at the end of the statement) asks it to find an exact match so if a non-existent part code is entered in E9 you will get an error message (**#N/A**).

Similarly, cell H9 holds the formula =VLOOKUP(E9,A4:C15,2) will return the VAT code relating to the part number.

Cell I11 holds a conditional (IF) function that will calculate VAT if the VAT code is 1 and insert 0 if the VAT code is 0.

Note that some cells have been formatted to show two decimal places and some to show no decimal places. Cell F2 is formatted as a percentage and, because

VAT might need to be changed, VAT is held in only one location with other cells referring to it.

Try out different part codes and quantities in the invoice.

CHANGES IN ASSUMPTIONS (WHAT-IF? ANALYSIS)

We referred earlier to the need to design a spreadsheet so that **changes in assumptions** do **not** require **major changes** to the spreadsheet. In our Cash Flow Exercise workbook we set up two separate areas of the spreadsheet, one for 20X6 assumptions and opening balances and one for the calculations and results. We could simply change the values in the assumptions cells to see how any changes in assumptions affect the results.

However, if we have more than one value to change, or we want to see the result of a number of different assumption changes we can use one of the three 'What-if' functions.

Data tables

A **data table** is a way to see different results by altering an input cell in a formula. You can create one- or two-variable data tables.

Let's try creating a one-variable data table.

(1) Open the earlier spreadsheet Mortgage which used the PMT formula

(2) Enter 1% to 10% in cells E8 to L8 as shown below:

(3) Select cells D8 to M9

(4) **Click Data>Table**

(5) Here you want your data table to fill in the values in row 9, based on the results if the value in cell C3 were to change to a different percentage, so choose the **Row input cell** box and enter C3

You should get the following results:

	1%	2%	3%	4%	5%	6%	7%	8%	9%	10%
-£193.00	-91.9789	-101.177	-110.92	-121.196	-131.991	-143.2862	-155.06	-167.288	-179.945	-193.004

The table would look better if the numbers were formatted in the same way as the first result in cell D9. An easy way to copy a format from one cell to another is to click on the cell whose format you wish to copy then click the **Format Painter** button on the standard toolbar and then click on the cells you wish to format.

Try it now. Click on cell D9, then click the **Format Painter** button. Now select cells E9:M9. You should see:

	1%	2%	3%	4%	5%	6%	7%	8%	9%	10%
-£193.00	-£91.98	-£101.18	-£110.92	-£121.20	-£131.99	-£143.29	-£155.06	-£167.29	-£179.95	-£193.00

Note. If you double click the **Format Painter** button you can then click any number of cells afterwards to apply that same format. To stop the **Format Painter**, simply click **Esc** (Escape).

Now let's try a two-variable data table using the same workbook. This time we want to see the result if both the interest rate and the number of years of the loan change.

(1) Rename the worksheet you have been working on to '1 variable'. Now select Sheet2 (or insert a new worksheet if necessary) and rename it '2 variables'. This is the sheet that we will now use.

(2) **Copy** the data on the One variable worksheet (**Ctrl + C**) and paste (**Ctrl + V**) into the new worksheet.

(3) Select cells E8 to M8 and move them up down by one cell (ie to E9 to M9). You can do this by hovering over the selected cells until a cross with four arrow heads appears, then click and drag to cell E9. Alternatively, **Cut** (**Ctrl + X**) and then **Paste** (**Ctrl + V**) to cell E9.

(4) In cells D10 to D14 insert different loan periods. We have used 10, 15, 20, 25 and 30 years as shown below:

-£193.00	1%	2%	3%	4%	5%	6%	7%	8%	9%	10%
10										
15										
20										
25										
30										

(5) Select cells D9 to M14

(6) **Click Data>Table**

(7) Here you want the data table to fill in the values based on the results if the value in cell C3 were to change to a different percentage (as shown in row 9) and also if the loan period in C5 changes (as shown in column D). So, choose the **Row input cell** box and enter C3 and then select the **Column input cell** box and enter C5.

You should get the following results:

-£193.00	1%	2%	3%	4%	5%	6%	7%	8%	9%	10%
10	-£175.21	-£184.03	-£193.12	-£202.49	-£212.13	-£222.04	-£232.22	-£242.66	-£253.35	-£264.30
15	-£119.70	-£128.70	-£138.12	-£147.94	-£158.16	-£168.77	-£179.77	-£191.13	-£202.85	-£214.92
20	-£91.98	-£101.18	-£110.92	-£121.20	-£131.99	-£143.29	-£155.06	-£167.29	-£179.95	-£193.00
25	-£75.37	-£84.77	-£94.84	-£105.57	-£116.92	-£128.86	-£141.36	-£154.36	-£167.84	-£181.74
30	-£64.33	-£73.92	-£84.32	-£95.48	-£107.36	-£119.91	-£133.06	-£146.75	-£160.92	-£175.51

You may need to use Format Painter to format the cells correctly.

Finally practice saving the file as 'Mortgage – Data tables' in a new folder on your computer using **Office button>Save as**. Choose an appropriate name for the folder – it's your choice! You can also open the file of that name from your CD.

Scenarios

The Scenarios function allows you to change information in cells that affect the final totals of a formula and to prepare instant reports showing the results of all scenarios together.

Using the spreadsheet Cash Flow Exercise – Finished, we will show the result of changing the following assumptions:

(a) Sales growth will only be 2% per month.

(b) Negotiations with suppliers and gains in productivity have resulted in cost of sales being reduced to 62% of sales.

(c) The effects of a recession have changed the cash collection profile so that receipts in any month are 50% of prior month sales, 35% of the previous month and 10% of the month before that, with bad debt experience rising to 5%.

You could simply change the relevant cells in the spreadsheet to reflect these changes in assumptions. However, we are going to use the Scenario Manager function.

(1) Select **Tools>Scenarios**

(2) Click **Add** and give the scenario an appropriate name, for example 'Original cash flow'

(3) Press the tab button or click in the **Changing cells** box and, based on the information we used above, select the cells with the changing data, ignoring the change to the opening bank balance. To select cells that are not next to each other, use the Ctrl button. You should **Ctrl click** on cells B7, B9, B10, B11 and G5.

(4) Click **OK**

(5) You are now asked for **Scenario Values**. This will show the values currently in the cells specified, which are our original figures so click **OK**

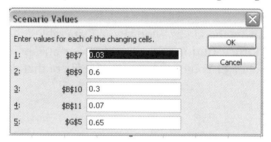

(6) We now need to enter our new values. Click **Add** and type a new **Name** (for example Cash Flow 2). The **Changing Cells** box will already contain the correct cells.

(7) Click **OK**.

(8) In the **Scenario Values** boxes change the values as follows and click **OK**

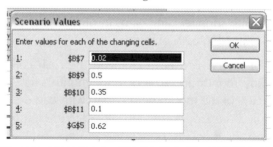

(9) Your second scenario should be highlighted. Now if you click on **Show** the figures in your assumptions table should automatically change and you can view the results.

	A	B	C	D	E	F	G	H
1	Cash flow projection: six months January - June 20X6							
2								
3	Assumptions/variables							
4								
5	Historical monthly sales 20X5 (£)	45,000		Purchases = cost of sales.			62%	of sales
6	Projected sales Jan 20X6 (£)	42,000		Monthly overheads 20X5 (£)			6,000	
7	Monthly sales growth (20X6 onwards)	2%		Rise in monthly overheads 20X6			5%	
8	Collection of debts:			Opening cash balance (O/d)			-7,500	
9	Month following sales	50%		Dividends (payable May 20X6, £)			10,000	
10	2nd month following sales	35%		Capital expenditure			18,000	
11	3rd month following sales	10%		Payable January			20%	
12	Uncollected	3%		Payable February			70%	
13				Payable May			10%	
14								
15	The cash flow							
16		Jan	Feb	Mar	Apr	May	Jun	
17		£	£	£	£	£	£	
18	Sales	42,000	42,840	43,697	44,571	45,462	46,371	
19	Cash receipts							
20	1 month in arrears	22,500	21,000	21,420	21,848	22,285	22,731	
21	2 months in arrears	15,750	15,750	14,700	14,994	15,294	15,600	
22	3 months in arrears	4,500	4,500	4,500	4,200	4,284	4,370	
23	Total operating receipts	42,750	41,250	40,620	41,042	41,863	42,701	
24								
25	Cash payments							
26	Purchases	26,040	26,561	27,092	27,634	28,187	28,750	
27	Overheads	6,300	6,300	6,300	6,300	6,300	6,300	
28	Total operating payments	32,340	32,861	33,392	33,934	34,487	35,050	
29								
30	Dividends					10,000		
31	Capital purchases	3,600	12,600			1,800		
32	Total other payments	3,600	12,600	0	0	11,800	0	
33								
34	Net cash flow	6,810	-4,211	7,228	7,109	-4,423	7,650	
35	Cash balance b/f	-7,500	-690	-4,901	2,327	9,436	5,012	
36	Cash balance c/f	-690	-4,901	2,327	9,436	5,012	12,663	

(10) Click back on your original cash flow scenario and then click **Show** and the numbers will change back

Note. You may need to make your screen smaller to view the whole sheet at the same time. You can do this by clicking **View** on the menu bar, then in the **Zoom** section clicking on **Zoom** and choosing a smaller percentage. 75% should be perfect. You can also do this by typing 75% directly into the **Zoom** box on the standard toolbar.

You can also easily and quickly create a report from the scenarios.

(1) Click **Tools>Scenarios>Summary**

(2) In the **Result cells** box choose the cells to go into the report, ie the ones you want to see the results of. As we are interested in the cash flow select cells B34:H34

This creates a separate **Scenario Summary** worksheet. Open the Cash Flow Exercise – What-if spreadsheet if you do not see the following report.

Scenario Summary			
	Current Values:	Original cash flow	Cash Flow 2
Changing Cells:			
B7	2%	3%	2%
B9	50%	60%	50%
B10	35%	30%	35%
B11	10%	7%	10%
G5	62%	65%	62%
Result Cells:			
B34	6,810	6,450	6,810
C34	-4,211	-5,169	-4,211
D34	7,228	6,443	7,228
E34	7,109	6,521	7,109
F34	-4,423	-4,894	-4,423
G34	7,650	7,302	7,650

Notes: Current Values column represents values of changing cells at time Scenario Summary Report was created. Changing cells for each scenario are highlighted in gray.

Goal seek

What if you already know the result you want from a formula but not the value the formula itself needs to calculate the result? In this case you should use the **Goal Seek** function, which is located in the **Data Tools** section of the **Data** tab on the Ribbon.

Open the original Mortgage spreadsheet from the downloaded files. Let's assume that we have enough income to pay a monthly mortgage payment of £300 and want to know how many years it will take to pay off the mortgage.

(1) Copy the data on Sheet1 and paste it to Sheet2

(2) Click **Tools>Goal Seek**

(3) **Set cell** to D9, as this is the figure we know and enter -300 in the **To value** box (make sure that you enter a negative figure to match the figure already in D9)

(4) Enter C5 in the **By changing cell** box, as this is the figure we are looking for

(5) Click **OK**

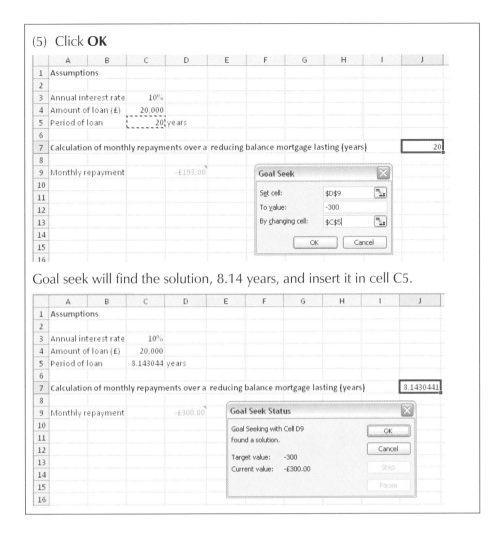

Goal seek will find the solution, 8.14 years, and insert it in cell C5.

STATISTICAL FUNCTIONS

Linear regression/trends

Excel contains powerful statistical tools for the analysis of information such as how costs vary with production volumes and how sales vary through the year.

Look at the following example of costs and volume:

Month	Volume	Costs £
1	1,000	8,500
2	1,200	9,600
3	1,800	14,000
4	900	7,000
5	2,000	16,000
6	400	5,000

It is clear that at higher production volumes costs are higher, but it would be useful to find a relationship between these variables so that we could predict what costs might be if production were forecast at, say, 1,500 units.

The first investigation that we could perform is simply to draw a graph of costs against volume. Volume is the independent variable (it causes the costs) so should run along the horizontal (x) axis.

Open the spreadsheet called Cost_volume and draw a scatter graph, using the data in cells B1:C7, showing cost against volume, with appropriate labels and legends.

Select **Insert>Chart** from the menu bar and choose the top left **Scatter** chart type.

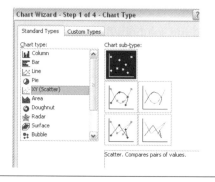

It should look something like the following:

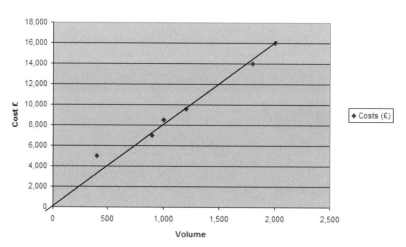

The straight line through the points has been manually drawn here to show that there's clearly a good association between volume and cost because the points do not miss the line by much, but we want to analyse this properly so that we can make a fairly good prediction of costs at output of say 1,500 units.

Lines of the sort above have a general equation of the type:

$$y = mx + b$$

Here y = total costs

x = volume

m = variable cost per unit (the slope of the line)

b = the fixed cost (where the line crosses the y axis: the cost even at zero volume)

Excel provides two easy ways of finding the figures we need for predicting values.

Find the trend:

(1)   On the same spreadsheet (Cost_volume), enter 1,500 in cell B9

(2)   Now click on cell C9

(3)   Choose **Insert>Function** then choose **Statistical** from the category list

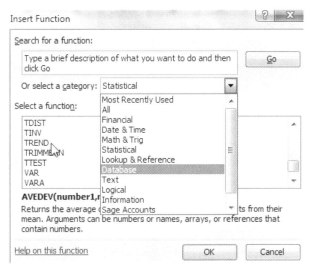

(4)   Scroll down the list until you get to **TREND** and choose that

(5)   For **Known_y's** select the range C2:C7

(6)   For **Known_x's** select the range B2:B7

(These ranges are the raw material which the calculation uses)

(7)   For **New_x's,** enter B9, the volume for which we want the costs to be predicted

The number 12,003 should appear in cell C9. That is the predicted cost for output of 1,500 units – in line with the graph. In practice, we would use 12,000. Altering the value in B9 will produce the corresponding predicted cost.

A second way of analysing this data will allow us to find the variable and fixed costs of the units (**m** and **b** in the equation **y** = **mx** +**b**).

---

(1) To find **m** use the statistical function **LINEST** and assign the **Known_y's** and **Known_x's** as before. You should get the answer 7.01, the variable cost per unit.

(2) To find the intersection, b, use the statistical function **INTERCEPT**. You should get the answer 1,486.

Note: These can be used to predict the costs of 1,500 units by saying:

Total costs = 1486 + 7.01 × 1,500 = 12,001, more or less as before.

The spreadsheet called Cost_volume finished contains the graph, and the three statistical functions just described.

Moving averages

Look at this data

Year	Quarter	Time series	Sales $'000
2006	1	1	989.0
	2	2	990.0
	3	3	994.0
	4	4	1015.0
2007	1	5	1030.0
	2	6	1042.5
	3	7	1036.0
	4	8	1056.5
2008	1	9	1071.0
	2	10	1083.5
	3	11	1079.5
	4	12	1099.5
2009	1	13	1115.5
	2	14	1127.5
	3	15	1123.5
	4	16	1135.0
2010	1	17	1140.0

You might be able to see that the data follows a seasonal pattern: for example there always seems to be a dip in Quarter 3 and a peak in Quarter 2. It is more obvious if plotted as a time series of sales against the consecutively numbered quarters.

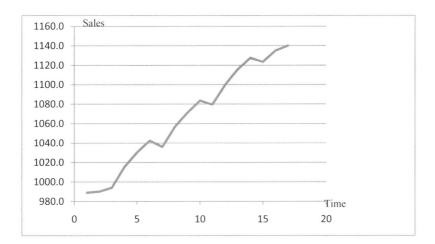

The moving average technique attempts to even out the seasonal variations. Here, because we seem to have data repeating every four readings a four-part moving average would be appropriate. If you were trading five days a week and wanted to even out the sales a five-part moving average would be suitable.

The moving average is calculated as follows:

Take the first four figures and average them:

$$\frac{(989.0 + 990.0 + 994.0 + 1,015.0)}{4} = 997.0$$

Then move on one season:

$$\frac{(990.0 + 994.0 + 1,015.0 + 1,030.0)}{4} = 1007.3$$

and so on, always averaging out all four seasons. Each average will include a high season and a low season.

That's rather tedious to do manually and Excel provides an function to do it automatically. To access this analysis function you must have the Excel Analysis ToolPak installed. If it is installed there will be a **Data Analysis** option in the **Tools** menu.

> If it is not installed, you can install it as follows:
>
> (1) Click the **Tools>Add-Ins**
>
> (2) Select the **Analysis ToolPak** check box, and then click **OK**
>
> **Tip**. If **Analysis ToolPak** is not listed in the **Add-Ins available** box, click **Browse** to locate it.
>
> If you are prompted that the **Analysis ToolPak** is not currently installed on your computer, click **Yes** to install it.

Open the spreadsheet called Time series.

(1) Select **Tools>Data analysis>Moving average**

(2) Select D2:D18 as the **Input Range**

(3) Enter 4 as the **Interval** (a four-part moving average)

(4) Enter F2 as the **Output Range**

(5) Check **Chart Output**

(6) Click on **OK**

Don't worry about the error messages – the first three simply mean that you can't do a four-part average until you have four readings.

Move your cursor onto the moving average figures and move it down, one cell at a time to see how the averages move.

Notice on the graph how the Forecast line (the moving average) is much smoother than the actual figures. This makes predicting future sales much easier.

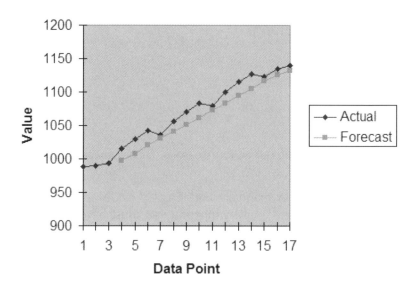

Moving Average

Mean, mode and median

These are three measures of what is known as the 'location' of data – they give an indication of whereabouts the data is clustered.

Mean (or arithmetic mean) is the ordinary average (add up the readings and divide by the number of readings).

Mode is the most frequently occurring item. For example, in a shoe shop, the arithmetic mean of shoe sizes is not much use. The shopkeeper is more interested in the most common shoe size.

Median is the value of the middle item if they are arranged in ascending or descending sequence. As well as medians you can have quartiles (upper and lower) dividing the population into top one-quarter, lowest three-quarters (or *vice versa*) and deciles (10:90 splits).

Excel allows all of these measures to be calculated (or identified) easily.

---

(1) Open the spreadsheet called Student results.

This lists the exam results of 23 students. They are currently displayed in alphabetical order. Don't worry about the column headed 'Bins' for now.

Enter 'Mean' in cell A28, then make cell B28 active.

(2) Choose **Σ>Average** and accept the range offered. 58.56 is the arithmetic mean of the marks

(3) Enter 'Median' in cell A29, then make cell B29 active

(4) Choose **Σ>More Functions>Statistical>MEDIAN**

(5) Enter the range B4:B26 for Number 1

You should see 57 as the median.

Check this by sorting the data into descending order by score, then counting up to the 12 student, Kate. (She's the middle student and scored 57.)

(6) Enter 'Percentile' in cell A30 and 0.75 in cell C30 and then make cell B30 active

(7) Choose **Σ>More Functions>Statistical>PERCENTILE**

(8) Enter the range B4:B26 and C30 as the K value

The reported value is 68, the figure which divides the top quarter from the bottom three-quarters of students.

(9) Enter 'Mode' in cell A31 then make cell B31 active

(10) Choose **Σ>More Functions>Statistical >Mode**

(11) Enter the range B4:B26

The reported value is 65 (that occurs more frequently than any other score).

Histograms

A histogram is a graph which shows the frequency with which certain values occur. Usually the values are grouped so that one could produce a histogram showing how many people were 160–165cm tall, how many >165–170, >170–175 and so on.

Excel can produce histogram analyses provided the Analysis ToolPak is installed. Installation was described earlier in the section about time series.

To demonstrate the histogram we will use the Student results spreadsheet again.

(1)   Open the Student results spreadsheet if it is not already open.

You will see that in E5 to E13 is a column called 'Bins'. This describes the groupings that we want our results to be included in, so here we are going up the result in groups (bins) of ten percentage points at a time and the histogram will show how many results are in 0–10, 10–20, 20–30 etc.

(2)   Choose **Tools>Data Analysis>Histogram**

(3)   Enter the range B4:B26 as the **Input Range**

(4)   Enter E5:E13 as the **Bin Range**

(5)   Choose **New Worksheet Ply** and enter 'Histogram analysis' in the white text box

(6)   Tick **Chart Output**

(7)   Click on **OK**

The new worksheet will show the data grouped into the 'bins' by frequency and also shows a histogram.

The spreadsheet 'Student results finished' shows the finished spreadsheet complete with histogram in the Histogram analysis sheet.

COMBINATION CHARTS

Excel allows you to combine two different charts into one. For example you may wish to compare sales to profits. This is also known as showing two graphs on one axis.

To do this we create a chart from our data as before.

(1) Open the Combination chart spreadsheet from the downloaded files. This provides data for the number of sales of precious metal in 2009 and 2010. The price at which the precious metal is sold per kilo goes up and down according to the market.

(2) Select the data that will go into your chart (cells A1 to C9)

(3) Click Insert and then choose your chart type. For this example let's choose a **2D clustered column** chart. The chart doesn't really help us to understand the relationship between the two different sets of data.

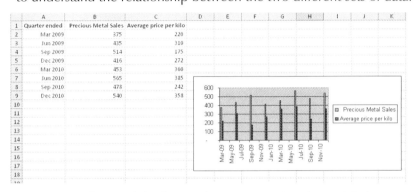

(4) A more visual way of displaying the average price data might be to see it in a line set against the number of sales. So click on any Average price column, right click and select **Chart Type.**

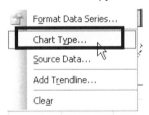

(5) Select **Line with Markers** and click **OK**. The chart will look like this:

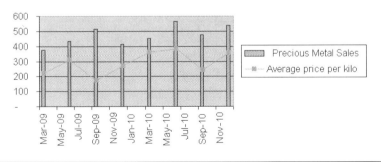

(6) The chart still does not make sense as the figures on the left axis are not comparing like with like. So we need to right click again an Average price marker and choose **Format Data Series**

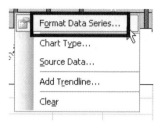

(7) Click on the **Axis** tab and choose **Secondary Axis**.

(8) Click **OK**.

(9) Take some time to play with the **Chart Options**. Give the chart the name 'Precious Metal Sales' and label the axes. The vertical axis on the left should show the 'Number of sales' so enter this label in the Value (Y) axis box. Enter 'Price per kilo' in the Second value (Y) axis box to add a label to the right hand axis.

You should end up with a chart that looks something like this:

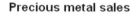

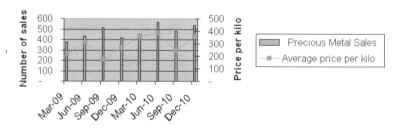

It can clearly be seen that the price per kilo dips in the third quarter of each year, something we could not easily determine without using the combination chart.

ERROR DETECTION AND CORRECTION

It is important to try to detect and correct errors before a spreadsheet is used to make decisions. We've already looked at some ways of trying to prevent wrong input (for example, data validation).

The final part of this chapter covers Excel's built-in help facility, error messages and ways to check that a spreadsheet has been constructed and is being used correctly.

Help

You can use Excel's Help window to quickly find the answer to any questions you may have while using Excel. You can access Help by clicking the **Help** button (the white question mark in the blue circle) at the end of the standard toolbar or by pressing **F1**.

You can also type a search term directly into the white bar at the end of the menu bar.

Take some time to explore the results when you type in different search terms. For example, if you found the section on What If analysis challenging, you could type 'What if' into the search bar to receive help on this topic.

Removing circular references

Circular references nearly always mean that there's a mistake in the logic of the spreadsheet. Here's an example:

	A	B
1		
2		£
3	Basic salary	20,000
4	Bonus 10% of total pay	=0.1*B5
5	Total pay	20,000

A warning will be displayed by Excel:

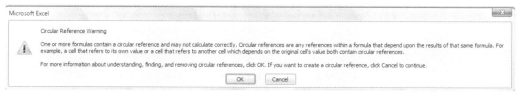

In our example, it is relatively easy to find the cause of the problem, but in a large spreadsheet it can be difficult. Clicking **OK** will provide help.

Using trace precedents

We saw earlier how to trace cells that provide data to a formula (precedents).

To recap, open the Precedent example 2 spreadsheet and click on cell D8. Then click **Tools>Formula Auditing>Trace Precedents**. A tracer arrow then appears linking the active cell with precedent cells.

	A	B	C	D
1				
2	£			
3	Region	Revenue	Costs	Gross profit
4	North	10,000	4,000	6,000
5	South	20,000	12,000	8,000
6	East	25,000	13,000	12,000
7	West	15,000	7,000	8,000
8		70,000	36,000	34,000

To identify the next level of precedents, remain in the active cell and select **Tools>Formula Auditing>Trace Precedents** again.

	A	B	C	D
1				
2	£			
3	Region	Revenue	Costs	Gross profit
4	North	10,000	4,000	6,000
5	South	20,000	12,000	8,000
6	East	25,000	13,000	12,000
7	West	15,000	7,000	8,000
8		70,000	36,000	34,000

Rounding errors

The ability to display numbers in a variety of formats (eg to no decimal places) can result in a situation whereby totals that are correct may actually look incorrect.

Example: rounding errors

The following example shows how apparent rounding errors can arise.

	A	B	C
1	Petty cash		
2	Week ending 31/12/20X6		
3			£
4	Opening balance		231.34
5	Receipts		32.99
6	Payments		-104.67
7	Closing balance		159.66

	A	B	C
1	Petty cash		
2	Week ending 31/12/20X6		
3			£
4	Opening balance		231
5	Receipts		33
6	Payments		-105
7	Closing balance		160

Cell B7 contains the formula =SUM(B4:B6). The spreadsheet on the left shows the correct total to two decimal places. The spreadsheet on the right seems to be saying that 231 + 33 105 is equal to 160, which is not true, it's 159 (check it). The **reason for the discrepancy** is that both spreadsheets actually contain the values shown in the spreadsheet on the **left**.

However, the spreadsheet on the right has been formatted to display numbers with **no decimal places**. So, individual numbers display as the nearest whole number, although the actual value held by the spreadsheet and used in calculations includes the decimals.

The Round Function

One solution, that will prevent the appearance of apparent errors, is to use the **ROUND function**. The ROUND function has the following structure: ROUND (value, places). 'Value' is the value to be rounded. 'Places' is the number of places to which the value is to be rounded.

The difference between using the ROUND function and formatting a value to a number of decimal places is that using the ROUND function actually **changes** the **value**, while formatting only changes the **appearance** of the value.

In the example above, the ROUND function could be used as follows. The following formulae could be inserted in cells D4 to D7.

    D4 = ROUND(C4,0)
    D5 = ROUND(C5,0)
    D6 = ROUND(C6,0)
    D7 = Round (SUM(D4:D6),0)

Column C could then be hidden by highlighting the whole column (click on the C at the top of the column), then select **Format>Column>Hide** from the main menu. Try this for yourself, hands-on.

D4			f_x =ROUND(C4.0)	
	A	B	D	E
1	Petty cash			
2	Week ending 31/12/20X6			
3				
4	Opening balance		231.0	
5	Receipts		33.0	
6	Payments		-105.0	
7	Closing balance		159.0	

Note that using the ROUND function to eliminate decimals results in slightly inaccurate calculation totals (in our example 160 is actually 'more correct' than the 159 obtained using ROUND. For this reason, some people prefer not to use the function, and to make users of the spreadsheet aware that small apparent differences are due to rounding.

Identifying error values

Error checking can be turned on by **Tools>Error checking>Options** and checking **Enable background error checking**. There is a list that allows you to decide which errors to be highlighted If a green triangle appears in a cell, then the cell contains an error.

#NUM!

Other information about the nature of the error will also be supplied:

#########	The column is not wide enough to hold the number. Widen the column or choose another format in which to display the number (no green triangle here as it is not a 'real' error – just a presentation problem.
#DIV>0!	Commonly caused by a formula attempting to divide a number by zero (perhaps because the divisor cell is blank).
#VALUE!	Occurs when a mathematical formula refers to a cell containing text, eg if cell A2 contains text the formula =A1+A2+A3 will return #VALUE!. Functions that operate on ranges (eg SUM) will not result in a #VALUE! error as they ignore text values.
#NAME?	The formula contains text that is not a valid cell address, range name or function name. Check the spelling of any functions used (eg by looking through functions under **Insert>Function**).
#REF!	The formula includes an invalid cell reference, for example a reference to cells that have subsequently been deleted. If you notice the reference immediately after a deletion, use **Ctrl+Z** to reverse the deletion.
#NUM!	This error is caused by invalid numeric values being supplied to a worksheet formula or function. For example, using a negative number with the **SQRT** (square root) function. To investigate, check the formula and function logic and syntax. The auditing toolbar may help this process (**View>Toolbars>Auditing Toolbar**).
#N>A	A value is not available to a function or formula, for example omitting a required argument from a spreadsheet function. Again, the **Auditing Toolbar** may help the investigation process.

Tracing and correcting errors

If you do see one of the above errors you can trace where it came from by clicking on the cell with the error, then, after activating the **Auditing Toolbar** (**View>Toolbars>Auditing Toolbar**) clicking the Trace Error button.

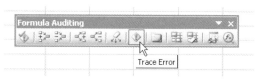

Lines will appear pointing to the data that has produced the error.

Clicking the **Error Checking** button (the first button on the toolbar) will automatically check the current worksheet and alert you to any errors.

Finally, you can click **Evaluate Formula** (the last button on the toolbar) to be taken step by step through it so that you can identify the error.

Note that you can also **Trace Precedents** and **Dependents** from the **Auditing Toolbar**.

CHAPTER OVERVIEW

- It is important to **backup your work regularly,** using **Save as** to give **different editions different names**.

- It is important to **control the security** of spreadsheets through passwords, locking (protecting) cells against unauthorised or accidental changes, data validation on input.

- Spreadsheet packages permit the user to work with **multiple sheets** that refer to each other. This is sometimes referred to as a three dimensional spreadsheet.

- Excel offers sophisticated data handling including **sorting, filtering, pivot tables** and **look-up tables.**

- **Combination charts** allow you to show two sets of data on one axis of your chart.

- Three tools, **Data tables, Scenarios** and **Goal seek,** are available to allow you to explore various results using different sets of values in one or more formulas.

- Error detection and prevention is important in spreadsheet design and testing. There are useful facilities available such as tracing precedents and dependents, identification of circular references, and error reports, , as well as Excel's built-in help function.

TEST YOUR LEARNING

Test 1

What command is used to save a file under a different name?

Test 2

What part of the menu do you go to set up checking procedures on the input of data?

Test 3

List three possible uses for a multi-sheet (3D) spreadsheet.

Test 4

What does filtering do?

Test 5

What is a trend line?

Test 6

What is the median?

PRACTICE ACTIVITIES

---
chapter coverage 📖

These activities enable you to practise some of the skills and techniques introduced in earlier chapters.

✍ The activities are suitable for both Excel 2003 and Excel 2007.

✍ Each activity requires you to create or open a specified spreadsheet with the suffix Question, eg Activity 1 Question.

✍ No printed answers are provided, but a spreadsheet which solves the problem will have a matching name with suffix Answer, eg Activity 1 Answer.

✍ The opening spreadsheets and answers for each activity are provided in the files available for download from **www.bpp.com/aatspreadsheets**.

✍ Some activities have no initial spreadsheet. The answer is a spreadsheet with the appropriate activity reference.

✍ The main coverage of each activity is set out below.

Contents

Question	Subject
1 Zumbo	Formatting
2 IML	Charts
3 Charge out (1)	General spreadsheet design
4 Charge out (2)	Amending a spreadsheet
5 Dittori	General spreadsheet design
6 Pivot	Pivot table
7 Rolling Projections Ltd	Large, general cash flow
8 Height and weight	Data manipulation and statistical functions
9 Retirement	Look-up and IF functions

1 ZUMBO

Open the spreadsheet Activity 1 Question.

	A	B	C	D	E
1	Zumbo Enterprises Ltd				
2					
3	Invoice				
4					
5	Date		40243		
6	Account		2141432		
7	Customer		J Jones		
8			21 The Cutting, Anytown AY1 2WF		
9					
10	Product cc	Product description	Quantity	Unit price	Net
11					£
12	1234	2 metre steel bar	10	12.33	123.3
13					0
14					0
15					0
16					0
17	Total net				123.3
18	VAT	0.175			21.5775
19	Total Gross				144.878

Layout needs to be improved so that the screen looks more like.

	A	B	C	D	E
1	**Zumbo Enterprises Ltd**				
2					
3	**Invoice**				
4					
5	Date		06 March 2010		
6	Account		2141432		
7	Customer		J Jones		
8			21 The Cutting, Anytown AY1 2WR		
9					
10	Product code	Product description	Quantity	Unit price	Net
11					£
12	1234	2 metre steel bar	10	12.33	123.30
13					0.00
14					0.00
15					0.00
16					0.00
17	Total net				123.30
18	VAT	17.50%			21.58
19	**Total Gross**				144.88
20					

Adjust font, borders, alignment, cell colour and number of decimal places to improve presentation.

2 IML

Open the spreadsheet Activity 2 Question.

	A	B	C	D	E
1	International Magazines Limited: Sales by Region Jan-Jun 2011				
2		Europe	America	Rest of the world	Total
3	Woman's Day	251,208	163,514	105,000	£ 519,722
4	Blue!	202,262	136,290	78,485	£ 417,036
5	Easy Cooking	143,588	86,040	114,900	£ 344,528
6	Sorted!	27,795	6,234	14,769	£ 48,798
7	Total	£624,852	£392,078	£313,154	£1,330,083

You work in the accounts department of International Magazines Limited (IML). IML publish four magazines, which are sold throughout the world. One of the spreadsheets you work on, shown above, analyses sales by magazine and world region.

Follow the instructions below to create several charts using the Chart Wizard.

(i)   Select cells **A2:D6** (ensure these are the only cells selected, do not include the totals).

(ii) Use the chart wizard button to insert three charts of that data: 2D clustered column, 2D stacked column and 3D clustered column.

(iii) Enter a suitable title for each graph.

(iv) Adjust their sizes and positions by obtaining the correct pointer shape, holding down the mouse button and dragging.

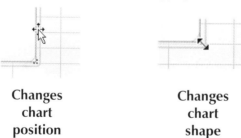

Changes
chart
position

Changes
chart
shape

3 CHARGE OUT (1)

You have been selected to work on a special assignment at a subsidiary company. The assignment team will consist of, besides you, the divisional chief accountant, an assistant accountant and a secretary. Because you are familiar with spreadsheets, you have been asked to set up a spreadsheet to record the time which each of you spends on this assignment and to cost it using your group's internal charge out rates, which are as follows.

	£
Divisional chief accountant	72.50
Assistant accountant	38.00
Accounting technician	21.45
Secretary	17.30

Tasks

Paying attention to **layout and good spreadsheet design principles** (for example, building in flexibility to allow for changes in charge out rates):

(a) Design a spreadsheet which will show hours spent and cost per person by week, and in total, for a three-week assignment.

(b) Complete the spreadsheet by entering the following time data, and calculate the total personnel costs of the job.

	Week 3	Week 2	Week 1
You	37 hrs 30 mins	40 hrs	32 hrs
Assistant accountant	35 hrs	40 hrs	20 hrs
Divisional chief accountant	6 hrs 45 mins	4 hrs 30 mins	–
Secretary	37 hrs 15 mins	32 hrs 15 mins	15 hrs

4 CHARGE OUT (2)

This activity uses the spreadsheet created in Activity 3.

A week later, back at head office, you receive a memo from the divisional chief accountant. He tells you that he has spent a further six hours on the assignment, in week 4. He also wants you to add in to your calculations the costs of two laptop computers which were charged out at £100 per week each for the duration of the three weeks of fieldwork. You have also found out that secretarial charge out rates were increased by 10% for all three weeks.

Amend the spreadsheet to reflect these changes.

5 DITTORI

Dittori Ltd has a sales ledger package which does not offer an aged debtors option. You have decided to set up a simple spreadsheet to monitor ageing by region. You have been able to export the following information from the sales ledger, as at 31 May 20X6. This data is contained in a spreadsheet – file Activity 5 Question.

Region	Current	1 month	2 month	3 month	4 month	5 month +
Highlands	346.60	567.84	32.17	–	–	54.8
Strathclyde	24,512.05	28,235.50	4,592.50	1,244.80	51.36	942.57
Borders	1,927.77	–	512.88	–	–	–
North West	824.80	14,388.91	2,473.53	–	482.20	79.66
North East	14,377.20	12,850.00	–	3,771.84	1,244.55	–
Midlands	45,388.27	61,337.88	24,001.02	4,288.31	1,391.27	4,331.11
Wales	14,318.91	5,473.53	21.99	4,881.64	512.27	422.5
East Anglia	157.20	943.68	377.40	1,500.87	15.33	247.66
South West	9,528.73	11,983.39	3,771.89	6,228.77	1,008.21	214.51
South East	68,110.78	83,914.54	29,117.96	24,285.10	14,328.90	5,422.50
France	6,422.80	7,451.47	5,897.55	2,103.70	140.50	3,228.76
Other EU	5,433.88	4,991.90	5,012.70	4,223.80	1,022.43	1,984.29
Rest of World	1,822.70	4,529.67	277.50	3,491.34	–	–

Task

Prepare a spreadsheet which will extend the above analysis to total debtors by region and the percentage of debt in each age category and the percentage by region.

6 PIVOT

Open the file Activity 6 Question. An extract from this spreadsheet is shown below.

	A	B	C	D
1	**Issue No**	**Quantity**	**Colour**	**Shape**
2	1473	159	Blue	Square
3	1474	84	Yellow	Square
4	1475	120	Green	Triangular
5	1476	125	Blue	Round
6	1477	153	Yellow	Triangular
7	1478	99	Blue	Round
8	1479	137	Blue	Triangular
9	1480	199	Red	Square
10	1481	16	Red	Round
11	1482	158	Green	Square
12	1483	29	Red	Triangular
13	1484	118	Yellow	Square
14	1485	167	Blue	Round
15	1486	177	Red	Triangular
16	1487	168	Green	Square
17	1488	110	Red	Round
18	1489	181	Red	Square
19	1490	168	Blue	Square
20	1491	31	Red	Square
21	1492	86	Green	Triangular
22	1493	160	Green	Triangular
23	1494	120	Red	Square
24	1495	101	Blue	Triangular
25	1496	141	Red	Triangular
26	1497	187	Blue	Triangular
27	1498	62	Green	Square
28	1499	177	Blue	Triangular
29	1500	148	Green	Square
30	1501	175	Red	Triangular
31	1502	131	Red	Square
32	1503	67	Blue	Square
33	1504	18	Blue	Round

The spreadsheet shows the quantity of components of various types that were issued from stores to production during a period. Components come in four colours (blue, red, green and yellow) and three shapes (square, round and triangular).

Task

Use Microsoft Excel's Pivot Table feature to analyse and summarise this data by colour and by shape in a two-dimensional table as shown below:

Sum of quantity	Colour				
Shape	Blue	Green	Red	Yellow	Grand total
Round					
Square					
Triangular					
Grand total					

7 ROLLING PROJECTIONS LTD

The accountant at Rolling Projections Ltd is preparing the cash flow forecast for the coming year. She has projected what she thinks the opening balance sheet (at 01 July 20X2) will be and wishes to prepare a 12-month (monthly) cash flow forecast for the following period.

The following information is relevant.

(a) Projected opening Balance Sheet

	£'000	£'000
Land and buildings	220	
Plant and machinery	110	
Motor vehicles	65	
		395
Inventory	40	
Trade debtors	60	
Cash in hand	5	
	105	
Overdraft	65	
Trade creditors	35	
	100	
Net current assets		5
Long-term creditors		120
Net assets		280
Share capital		100
Reserves		180
		280

(b) Budgeted Profit and Loss Account for the year ending 30 June 20X3

	£'000
Revenue	390
Cost of sales	165
Rent and rates	60
Depreciation	30
Marketing	35
Administrative expenses	75
Selling expenses	45
Loss before interest	20

(c) One-sixth of the year's sales occur in each of the months of July and August. The rest are evenly spread over the remaining months of the year. Debtor balances are usually collected as follows:

(i)   10% in the month of sale
(ii) 60% in the month following sale
(iii) 30% in the second month after sale

The accountant expects to be able to collect 90% of opening debtor balances in July and will write-off the rest.

(d)   Trade creditors are paid 20% in the month of purchase and 80% in the following month. Because she ran a large batch of cheques just before year-end, the accountant does not expect to have to settle opening trade creditors until August.

The accountant is budgeting for no overall change in inventory levels. Purchases are spread evenly over the year.

(e)   Rates, which total £20,000, are paid in April, and rent (the balance on the rent and rates account) is paid in equal amounts on 25 March, 24 June, 29 September and 25 December.

(f)   The marketing budget is set at £1,000 per month excluding November. The balance will be spent on a major burst campaign in November.

(g)   Administrative expenses are spread evenly over the year.

(h)   Selling expenses are paid in the month of sale and are incurred in the same proportion as that in which sales are earned.

(i)   Interest of 2% per month is paid on any overdraft balance at the end of the month and added to the account balance. (**Hint.** Use an IF statement).

(j)   Cash in hand is not to be included in opening bank balances for the purpose of this projection.

Task

(a)   Prepare a monthly cash flow forecast for the year ending 30 June 20X3.

Pay attention to layout and to making the spreadsheet flexible to accommodate changes in assumptions.

(b)   Using the Chart Wizard prepare a column chart showing, for each month, total receipts, total payments and net receipts/payments.

Hint. You can select the three ranges of data by selecting the first, holding down the Ctrl key, selecting the second, then still holding down the Ctrl key, select the third.

8 HEIGHT AND WEIGHT

The spreadsheet Activity 8 Question contains data about a number of people's height and weight. Open that spreadsheet. The data is presently in alphabetical order by name of person.

Tasks

Just below the list of data use **statistical functions** to work out:

(a) Mean height and mean weight (175.56, 70.3).

(b) Number of people in the sample (25).

(c) Minimum height and minimum weight (169, 58.2).

(d) Maximum height and maximum weight (182, 84.5).

(e) Mode for height and mode for weight (the most common readings, 175, 67.4).

(f) Median for height and median for weight (the middle reading, 175, 70.1).

(g) Sort the table of data by height and check the mode and median obtained for height.

(h) Sort the table of data by weight and check the mode and median obtained for weight.

(i) Draw a scatter graph of weight (y) against height (x).

(j) Use the Trend function to estimate, to one decimal place, the weight of someone who is 175.5 cm tall (70.2 kgs).

(k) Set up a bin range on your spreadsheet with values of 169, 170,....182, and produce a histogram for heights.

9 RETIREMENT

Open the spreadsheet Activity 9 Question.

	A	B
	Activity 1 Question	
1	Retirement age	65
2		
3	Name	Vic
4	Age	
5		
6	Years to retirement	
7		
8		
9	Name	Age
10	Annette	38
11	Josephine	43
12	Mike	32
13	Paula	70
14	Vandana	42
15	Omar	34
16	Vic	66
17		

In B4 insert a VLOOKUP function which will display the age of the person whose name is typed into cell B3.

In B6 insert the number of years to retirement (with reference to the value in B1). If the person has reached retirement age or is older B6 should state 'Retired'.

AAT SAMPLE SPREADSHEET CASE STUDY

This case study is in two parts. All spreadsheets should be titled and contain a footer with your name, date and AAT registration number. You are required to open or download existing spreadsheet (from the internet or from a memory stick provided by your assessor) for some of these tasks.

It is called "Spreadsheet data for the AAT sample assessment" and it comprises of various worksheets within the workbook.

Answers to Parts 1 and 2 are available for download. Type **www.bpp.com/aatspreadsheets** into your web browser.

*You have **one and a half hours** to complete the tasks and a high degree of accuracy is required.*

PART ONE

JA Muddlestone is a wholesaler of surplus stocks, which they resell to small traders, either via the sales team or over the internet on EBid. You are employed as an accounts clerk in the company. The computer system has crashed and the back up will not load due to a technical problem.

The accountant has asked you to collate some figures into a spreadsheet to give an overview of the activity for the last year

Over the past year the monthly results have been as follows

Sales

January	£42,980
February	£55,980
March	£92,600
April	£118,206
May	£117,420
June	£120,115

You have discovered that the expenses for each month were as follows:

January	£15,390
February	£23,602
March	£28,750
April	£35,060
May	£37,420
June	£38,790

The information about the cost of sales is listed below:

January	£14,620	February	£17,940	March	£21,405
April	£29,800	May	£30,650	June	£34,020

Task one

(1a) Prepare a spreadsheet, showing all the above figures. Formulate cells for January to show gross profit and net profit then copy these formulas into the remaining cells. Gross profit is sales less cost of sales, and net profit is gross profit less expenses. (Months should be in column A, with January in cell A5, sales, expenses, cost of sales, gross profit, net profit should then be put into columns B, C ,D, E & F respectively.)

(1b) Use formulae to total each column.

(1c) Label columns G and H gross profit margin and net profit margin, respectively. Gross profit margin is calculated as gross profit expressed as a percentage of sales and net profit margin as net profit expressed as a percentage of sales, and use formula to calculate theses figures for each month (as a percentage rounded to two decimal places).

(1d) Title this as J A Muddlestone (cell A1) Monthly figures for 2009 (cell A2) and Save as worksheet JAM 1.

Task two

Open the EBid worksheet

(2a) Open a new worksheet and copy the information from the EBID worksheet. Give this the title Ebid History using font size 16 for the title, centred on the page.

Format headers to bold and ensure column widths and row heights are suitable. Then use the spellcheck function to check and resolve any errors.

(2b) Insert a row between books and collectables, type 'coins' in cell A6 and type '1910 shilling' in cell B6. Input bids 1 to 12 of £5, £15, £75, £180, £200, £195, £215, £465, £320, £299, £450 and £445, respectively.

(2c)   Insert three new columns between columns B & C and label these "lowest bid", "average bid" and "highest bid", and enter the necessary formulae to calculate the additional columns.

(2d)   Change the format of all numerical cells to currency rounded to the nearest £ and use conditional formula to change cell content to a light red fill with dark red text of the highest bid for the JP computers category on the worksheet.

(2e)   Produce a line chart, to show the bid history of JP computers and save this. Insert the line chart below the bid figures, ensuring it is appropriately labelled and has a suitable title.

(2f)   Save spreadsheet as JAM-BID1 and print, ensuring the data and graph will print onto one sheet of A4 (Please note that no actual print will occur, but this activity will be recorded by the computer).

PART TWO

Parkins Cars are a large car dealership, selling a range of luxury cars and accessories.

Open the sales commission data for Parkins Cars (there are two worksheets for this, Saleforce results and % commission rates).

Task one

Copy and paste the Parkins salesforce worksheet into a new worksheet and then use this, and the data in the other worksheet

(1a)   Insert formulae to calculate:

(i)   The total value of sales for each sales person

(ii)   The commission earned by each sales person on each car make (to two decimal places)

(iii) The total commissions earned by each sales person

(iv)   The total value of sales and commission, for each car make and the total of all sales and commissions paid

(1b)   Format the spreadsheet with

- Titles in bold
- Use currency to two decimal places
- Adjust column width as necessary

(1c)   Sort the spreadsheet alphabetically by family name order.

(1d)   Save the worksheet with the file name "Parkinsalphalist"

(1e) Copy the information from "Parkinsaphalist" to a new worksheet. Using the new worksheet, use formula to calculate the average value of total sales per sales person.

(1f) If total sales for any individual sales person are more than 20 per cent above the average figure then a bonus of one per cent of their total sales figure should be given. Calculate this bonus, where applicable. Calculate totals of all commissions and bonuses to be paid to each sales person.

(1g) Rank the spreadsheet by total sales from the lowest value to the highest value. Save as worksheet with file name "Parkinsranked".

Task two

Parkins Motors also sell a range of car accessories. These are sold in the showrooms, across the internet and from their own catalogue.

Open "Parkins accessories" worksheet and copy this data to a new worksheet.

(2a) Create a pivot table to show the total revenue from each type of sales. The pivot table should be displayed to the right of the data provided, and saved as Parkins accessories.

Task three

Short answer questions

Insert your answers into the "Parkins accessories" worksheet and save your work.

(i) If you wanted to visually compare sales information on a month by month basis what type of chart would you use?

A   Bar chart
B   Pie chart
C   Gantt chart
D   Histogram

(ii) Which of these is a spreadsheet tool you could use to identify an error in a formula.

A   Conditional formatting
B   Spellcheck
C   Error checking
D   Error formatting

TEST YOUR LEARNING ANSWERS

CHAPTER 1 Introduction to spreadsheets (Excel 2007)

1 Text, values or formulae.

2 F5 opens a GoTo dialogue box which is useful for navigating around large spreadsheets. F2 puts the active cell into edit mode.

3 You can use the technique of 'filling' – selecting the first few items of a series and dragging the lower right corner of the selection in the appropriate direction.

4 Select Formulas on the Ribbon then click Show Formulas. Alternatively press Ctrl + `.

5 Removing gridlines, adding shading, adding borders, using different fonts and font sizes, presenting numbers as percentages or currency or to a certain number of decimal places.

6 =IF(logical test, value if true, value if false)

7 (a) =Sum(B4:B5) or =B4+B5
   (b) =Sum(B5:D5)
   (c) =Sum(E4:E5) or =Sum(B6:D6) or best of all to check for errors:

   =IF(SUM(E4:E5)= Sum(B6:D6), Sum(B6:D6),"Error")

8 (a)   =SUM(B4:B8)
   (b)   =C9*D1
   (c)   =D9+D10 or =D9*(1+D1)

CHAPTER 2 More advanced spreadsheet techniques (Excel 2007)

1   Save as

2   Data > Data Validation

3   The construction of a spreadsheet model with separate Input, Calculation and Output sheets. They can help consolidate data from different sources. They can offer different views of the same data.

4   Filtering allows you to see only areas of a table where there are certain values. Other items are filtered from view.

5   The trend line shows how one variable (for example cost) increases as another does (eg volume of production).

6   If data is ranked in ascending or descending order the median is the value of the middle item.

CHAPTER 3 Introduction to spreadsheets (Excel 2003)

1   Text, values or formulae.

2   F5 opens a GoTo dialogue box which is useful for navigating around large spreadsheets. F2 puts the active cell into edit mode.

3   You can use the technique of 'filling' – selecting the first few items of a series and dragging the lower right corner of the selection in the appropriate direction.

4   Select Tools, Options, ensure the View tab is active then tick the Formulas box within the window options area.

5   Removing gridlines, adding shading, adding borders, using different fonts and font sizes, presenting numbers as percentages or currency or to a certain number of decimal places.

6   =IF(logical test, value if true, value if false)

7   (a)   =Sum(B4:B5) or =B4+B5
    (b)   =Sum(B5:D5)
    (c)   =Sum(E4:E5) or =Sum(B6:D6) or best of all to check for errors: =IF(SUM(E4:E5)= Sum(B6:D6), Sum(B6:D6),"Error")

8   (a)   =SUM(B4:B8)
    (b)   =C9*D1
    (c)   =D9+D10 or =D9*(1+D1)

CHAPTER 4 More advanced spreadsheet techniques (Excel 2003)

1   Save as

2   Data > Validation

3   The construction of a spreadsheet model with separate Input, Calculation and Output sheets. They can help consolidate data from different sources. They can offer different views of the same data.

4   Filtering allows you to see only areas of a table where there are certain values. Other items are filtered from view.

5   The trend line shows how one variable (for example cost) increases as another does (eg volume of production).

6   If data is ranked in ascending or descending order the median is the value of the middle item.

INDEX

Notes

Notes

Notes

Notes

Notes

REVIEW FORM

How have you used this Workbook?
(Tick one box only)

☐ Home study

☐ On a course_____

☐ Other _____

Why did you decide to purchase this Workbook? *(Tick one box only)*

☐ Have used BPP Texts in the past

☐ Recommendation by friend/colleague

☐ Recommendation by a college lecturer

☐ Saw advertising

☐ Other _____

During the past six months do you recall seeing/receiving either of the following?
(Tick as many boxes as are relevant)

☐ Our advertisement in Accounting Technician

☐ Our Publishing Catalogue

Which (if any) aspects of our advertising do you think are useful?
(Tick as many boxes as are relevant)

☐ Prices and publication dates of new editions

☐ Information on Text content

☐ Details of our free online offering

☐ None of the above

Your ratings, comments and suggestions would be appreciated on the following areas of this Workbook.

	Very useful	Useful	Not useful
Introductory section	☐	☐	☐
Quality of explanations	☐	☐	☐
Chapter tasks	☐	☐	☐
Chapter Overviews	☐	☐	☐
Test your learning	☐	☐	☐
Index	☐	☐	☐

	Excellent	Good	Adequate	Poor
Overall opinion of this Workbook	☐	☐	☐	☐

Do you intend to continue using BPP Products?   ☐ Yes   ☐ No

Please note any further comments and suggestions/errors on the reverse of this page. The author of this edition can be e-mailed at: suedexter@bpp.com

Please return to: Sue Dexter, Publishing Director, BPP Learning Media Ltd, FREEPOST, London, W12 8BR.

REVIEW FORM (continued)

TELL US WHAT YOU THINK

Please note any further comments and suggestions/errors below.